Feel Beauty Full

7 Steps to Allowing Natural Beauty

One woman's interpretation of the teachings of Abraham

By Sarah Crowley

BALBOA.
PRESS
A DIVISION OF HAY HOUSE

Interior Graphics/Art Credit: Joanna K. Dane

Balboa Press books may be ordered through booksellers or by contacting:

Balboa Press
A Division of Hay House
1663 Liberty Drive
Bloomington, IN 47403
www.balboapress.com
1 (877) 407-4847

Because of the dynamic nature of the Internet, any web addresses or links contained in this book may have changed since publication and may no longer be valid. The views expressed in this work are solely those of the author and do not necessarily reflect the views of the publisher, and the publisher hereby disclaims any responsibility for them.

The author of this book does not dispense medical advice or prescribe the use of any technique as a form of treatment for physical, emotional, or medical problems without the advice of a physician, either directly or indirectly. The intent of the author is only to offer information of a general nature to help you in your quest for emotional and spiritual well-being. In the event you use any of the information in this book for yourself, which is your constitutional right, the author and the publisher assume no responsibility for your actions.

Print information available on the last page.

ISBN: 978-1-5043-7652-5 (sc)
ISBN: 978-1-5043-7654-9 (hc)
ISBN: 978-1-5043-7653-2 (e)

Library of Congress Control Number: 2017903874

Balboa Press rev. date: 07/26/2017

Dedicated to my mom, the most beautiful woman in my universe.

If the present moment has peace and joy and
happiness,
then the future will have also.

~Thich Nhat Hanh

With deep appreciation for Esther and Jerry Hicks,
Abraham,
Robert,
and all of the co-creators of my beauty full life.

7 Steps to Allowing Natural Beauty

Step 1:
Think Thoughts That Feel Good

Step 2:
Meditate

Step 3:
Breathe Deeply

Step 4:
Nourish Yourself

Step 5:
Recognize Your Worthiness

Step 6:
Take Responsibility For Your Feelings

Step 7:
Laugh Often

Contents

The intention of this body of work is to uplift.
If it doesn't feel that way to you, feel free to put it down
and find something else to do that feels good. Come
back to it another day. Or don't. Just do what feels
good to you.

"It feels good to feel good."
~Abraham

A few years ago, along with millions of other people, I watched "The Secret" introduced on Oprah. I started to watch the episode, and quickly paused it, realizing that this was one of the few shows that I would wait to watch with Robert, my husband.
It felt important.
We watched it together later that evening, and, like many others I'm sure, our lives changed.

More accurately, they shifted.
Ultimately, "The Secret" introduced us to a new understanding of the law of attraction and, in turn, a variety of teachers; most notably, Abraham, upon whose teachings "The Secret" is based. (Nope, not the guy from the Old Testament. Check out www. abraham-hicks.com for more information.) Over the course of the following years, Robert and I attracted the teachings of Deepak Chopra, Eckhart Tolle, Wayne Dyer, Maharishi Mahesh Yogi, Jill Bolte Taylor, Don Miguel Ruiz, Swami Vivikananda, B. K.S. Iyengar, as well as many others. I had always considered myself "a seeker," someone who is drawn to and interested in the many forms of spirituality. But I had never understood it more clearly than when I was introduced to the law of attraction:

Your thoughts create your reality.

Rather quickly, life made a lot more sense to Robert and I. We were both in awe of the simple truth taught by Abraham, that nothing is more important than that you feel good. When you choose to make feeling good your dominant intention, ease and effortlessness will be more and more present in your life.

And living with ease and effortlessness is a pretty remarkable way to live.

First of All...

Natural Beauty

Allow me to explain what I mean by "natural beauty."

Natural beauty has nothing to do with how you look, and everything to do with how you feel.

When you feel good, you are beauty full, and you exude natural beauty.

Natural beauty is the glow from within that attracts people to those who possess it. Conventional beauty lies on the surface and is determined by DNA and cultural ideals. It is enhanced by your clothes, make-up, hairstyle, and whatever other factors you choose. Natural beauty reflects the heart, the brain, and the mind; not the face, the hair and the body.

Natural beauty lies within our consciousness and is attainable by anyone who has the mindset of allowing Well-Being. It is far more powerful and alluring to achieve beauty at this level.

Natural beauty is about radiating beauty. Natural beauty is inner confidence - wholeheartedness, an understanding of your worthiness, a willingness to embrace vulnerability and uncertainty. And this is possible for anyone, once you have an understanding of who you really are.

"The infinite library of the universe is in your own mind."
~Swami Vivikenanda

Who am I?

Some people ask themselves this question often, while others have never even considered it. Many people would probably come up with an answer like "a mother," "a lawyer," "Sarah," and so forth. But I'm not asking, "what label are you?" Labels are created by our ego, a pea-sized portion of our left-brain that dictates who we are as an individual. I ask you to consider who you *really* are. To look beyond the labels assigned by your ego, and find the truth:

I am.

I am consciousness. I am energy. I am vibration.

What do I mean by consciousness, energy and vibration? I mean that you are a part of the unified field of consciousness that has literally created the universe. You are as much a part of this field of consciousness as a wave is a part of an ocean. You are everything, because the greater part of you is non-physical, fluid energy. All matter is energy at its core, which means that you, too, are more energy than matter. And the beautiful thing is that the study of quantum physics has proven this to be true.

"In the 1920's, the physicist Werner Heisenburg (and other founders of the science of quantum mechanics) made a discovery so strange that the world has yet to completely come to terms with it. When observing sub-atomic phenomena, it is impossible to completely separate the observer (that is, the scientist making the experiment) from what is being observed. In our day-to-day world, it is easy to miss this fact. We see the universe as a place full of separate objects (tables and chairs, people and planets) that occasionally interact with each other, but that nonetheless remain essentially separate. On the sub-atomic level, however, this universe of separate objects turns out

to be a complete illusion. In the realm of the super-super small, every object in the physical universe is intimately connected with every other object. In fact, there are really no 'objects' in the world at all, only vibrations of energy, and relationships."
(Eben Alexander - Proof of Heaven)

Consider this: each of our 50 trillion cells are made of molecules. Molecules are made of atoms. Atoms are made of sub-atomic particles. And sub-atomic particles are not *made* of energy, they *are* energy. The idea that "we are energy" is not just another belief. A common phrase used by Abraham is also a scientifically proven fact:

"We are vibrational beings in a vibrational universe."

We have 50 trillion cells in our bodies, each a packet of energy vibrating on a sub-atomic level.

We *are* energy.

This all-encompassing energy is purely positive. It is Well-Being. There is no negativity. Negativity is a reflection of our resistance to the Well-Being that is always there. When you are feeling anger, frustration, fear, any negative emotion, it is an indication that you have ceased to allow the Well-Being that is always flowing. Release the resistance, and you will feel good again.

This Well-Being, or pure positive energy, is who we really are. It is our consciousness, the non-physical part of ourselves. You can call it Well-Being, Source Energy, the soul, God. It is always there and we are all a part of it - we *are* it.

We *are* Well-Being, Source Energy, the soul, God.

In Dying To Be Me, while describing her near-death experience, Anita Moorjani writes, "And then I was overwhelmed by the realization that God isn't a being [God, Krishna, Buddha, Jesus], but *a state of being... and I was now that state of being.*"

When you make the connection that this energy that created the stars and the planets and all life on earth is who you really are, you can begin to create anything in your life - including natural beauty.

The Law of Attraction

"The moment I realize God sitting in the temple of
every human body, the moment I stand in reverence before
every human being and see God in him or her, in that
moment everything that binds me vanishes
and I am free."
~Swami Vivikenanda

As the old saying goes, with God, everything is possible.
Not some things, everything. Understand that there
is no distinction between your true self and Source
Energy. Recognize that you have infinite creativity. *You*
are the powerful creator of your own reality.

Everything that constitutes your physical reality begins
in your mind, whether you are aware of it or not. We're
creating deliberately or we're creating in-deliberately,
but we're always creating. The basic premise of the law
of attraction is that "like attracts like." Once you are able
to make the connection between what you think about
and how you feel, dramatic shifts in your life will unfold.

Many people have a misconstrued notion of the law
of attraction, if they've heard of it at all, believing
"think positively and get lots of stuff." Really, the law of
attraction is just the answer to the question of how our
thoughts create our reality.

In <u>Transcendental Meditation</u>, Jack Forem explains,
"Thoughts are not just mental abstractions...They have
a physical side; the thinking brain (and the dreaming
brain, too) emits faint pulses of electrical energy that
can be detected and measured."

Our thoughts are energy.
Our thoughts are vibration.

We react to our thoughts with emotions, and those emotions are indicators of what kind of thoughts we are thinking. In turn, our emotions are indicators of the vibrations we are emitting into the universe. We're either thinking good feeling thoughts (which vibrate at a high frequency), and attracting situations that continue to make us feel good, or bad feeling thoughts (which vibrate at a low frequency), and attracting situations that continue to make us feel bad. The sooner you move in the direction of thoughts that feel good the better, as that will be your point of attraction.

When we feel good, or experience emotions such as joy, happiness, hope, appreciation and love, we are vibrating at a high frequency. Because the law of attraction dictates that like attracts like, when you vibrate at a high frequency, the universe has no choice but to bring you more high frequency situations, more things that will make you feel good, and be a match to the vibration you are emitting. Good feelings radiate positive vibrations, and attract positivity, happiness, and beauty into your life. This is why Abraham likes to say, "the better it gets, the better it gets!"

On the other hand, bad feeling thoughts lead to negative emotions such as anger, frustration, fear, and worry. When you are in this state of mind, you are attracting more of these bad feeling situations. If you've ever started your day (or month, or year) on "the wrong side of the bed," and your whole day (or month, or year) continues to "go wrong," you've experienced the law of attraction at work.

Until you shift your thoughts,
and, in turn,
your feelings,
and, in reality,
your vibration,
you will continue to attract similar bad feeling
situations.

Keep in mind - the law of attraction will always present you with evidence to support whatever it is that you're thinking. That's the funny thing. If you think that the law of attraction isn't real, the law of attraction will show you evidence that it is not real. Confusing? Maybe. But true. People don't question the law of gravity because it is tangible. Without it, we'd be floating around in space. The law of attraction isn't as tangible, but it is just as active. From a scientific standpoint, it is indisputable:

We are vibrational beings in a vibrational universe, and like attracts like.

In order to use the law of attraction to your benefit, instead of "thinking positively," think thoughts that *feel* good, because it's the *feeling* that indicates the *vibration* that will bring more of the same feeling or vibration.

Once you make the connection between what you are thinking, how you are feeling, and the experiences you are living, you can begin to create your life *deliberately*, exactly as you want it to be.

STEP ONE

Think Thoughts That Feel Good

"Nothing is more important than that you feel good."

~Abraham

When you make the choice to believe that nothing is more important than feeling good, you are choosing to be a deliberate creator of a happy, effortless existence. How do you make that happen?
The simple answer is: think thoughts that feel good.

Consider, from a scientific standpoint, how your thoughts affect your physical body. When you think a thought, your body reacts with a physiological response. Depending on the thought you are thinking, your heart rate may increase, tears may come to your eyes, you may blush, and so on - the physical reactions we experience as a result of our thoughts are endless. We call such reactions our emotions.

Again, emotions are indicators of our point of attraction. In order to use the law of attraction to your benefit, it is necessary to shift your vibration by thinking better feeling thoughts. "Thinking positively" can be difficult when you're angry. Instead, the goal is to be consistently moving up what Abraham would call the "vibrational scale of emotions." Any thought that brings you relief from where you are right now is the answer, as the feeling of relief will begin to shift the momentum from feeling lousy to feeling better.

The "Vibrational Scale of Emotions,"
as described by Abraham in their book
Ask And It Is Given:

1. Joy/Knowledge/Empowerment/Freedom/Love/Appreciation
2. Passion
3. Enthusiasm
4. Positive Expectation/Belief
5. Optimism
6. Hopefulness
7. Contentment
8. Boredom
9. Pessimism
10. Frustration/Irritation/Impatience
11. Overwhelment
12. Disappointment
13. Doubt
14. Worry
15. Blame
16. Discouragement
17. Anger
18. Revenge
19. Hatred/Rage
20. Jealousy
21. Insecurity/Guilt/Unworthiness
22. Fear/Grief/Depression/Despair/Powerlessness

"I love anger. Angry people are just more empowered sad people."
~Panache Desai, Discovering Your Soul Signature

My Mom Is Not Afraid of Her Arms

Over the course of my career, I have worked with countless women who have issues with their bodies. Truly, too many to count. Beautiful women who are unhappy with the way that they look. Nine times out of ten, these women think they are overweight. And/or they think something on their bodies is unattractive. For instance, I've determined that if you are a woman, over 45, and living in the USA, you hate your upper arms. To me, and most of the world, your arms look beautiful.
They are feminine.
They are arms.
There's nothing wrong with them.

I don't think that I've been able to convince a single woman that their arms look just fine, and that she should go ahead and wear that sleeveless top. (Superficial example perhaps, but you get the picture.) It's difficult to change someone's perception of themselves or their body. That change has to come from within.
It is possible to feel good about yourself.
To feel good in general.
To feel beautiful.

I believe that we all want to feel beautiful. To some extent, everyone cares about how they look. There is nothing wrong with that. We live in these bodies 24/7 - it would be difficult *not* to care about our appearance. Fortunately, it's not about *changing our appearance* to reflect society's constrictive standard of beauty. Instead, we can *change the way we feel* about ourselves. When we change our *perspective* regarding our bodies and our beauty to reflect feeling good, we begin to transform our lives. This isn't about being superficial. This is about learning how to love and appreciate ourselves.

If you asked me whether I have my own issues with my body, the answer would be, sometimes, hands down, yes. However, I have learned that when I focus on what I do like about my body, I feel good. And when I'm in a state of acceptance of - and appreciation for - my body, I feel good, and healthy habits come naturally.

We get to choose how we feel about everything, including how we look. It has nothing to do about how we look to others, or about wanting others to think we're beautiful. It's *our own* perception that matters.

If beauty is in the eye of the beholder, the beholder is YOU.

So I tell myself that I want to feel good about myself, about my body, and everything, really. Be willing to see yourself from a place of love and acceptance. Like my mom, who has old-lady arms but still wears sleeveless tops. See your beauty. Feel beauty full.

Perception Is Everything

I once saw a television show that I found truly inspiring -
Carson Kressley's "How To Look Good Naked." At the
beginning of every show, Carson yelled, "We need a
perception revolution!"
"Thank you!" I yelled back to the screen.
If we perceive ourselves from a negative light,
the universe can only offer us a reflection of that
perception. Change your perception to encompass
your beauty, and you will be beautiful. It may be
difficult to believe, but as Abraham teaches, "a belief is
just a thought you keep thinking."

Body image: the image we have of our own bodies is
our perception, and our perception of ourselves is what
really matters. Because more often than not, how we
feel about our bodies has nothing to do with reality.
It's about how we *think* we look.
Most of us are perfectly healthy, no matter our size
or weight. But we still so often think of ourselves as
"fat" or "overweight" or "not right" for some reason or
another. And why? Because we're comparing ourselves
to America's Next Top Schmodel? Pretty much.

We all know how much we're bombarded with
unrealistic expectations of beauty. But who is really
setting the expectation? It's not the beauty industry.
It's YOU. We constantly compare ourselves to others,
yet we are here to live a unique experience in our own
unique bodies, which are all sorts of different shapes
and sizes. With the comparisons come the negative
thoughts regarding our bodies, followed by the *warped
perception* of our physical selves.

We see flaws where others don't. We are our harshest critics. What if we made the choice to be kinder to ourselves? To start loving and appreciating our bodies, whatever state they are in?
Even if you are obese? Or very thin?
Especially if you are.
Because no matter where you are physically, once you begin, or decide, to unconditionally love yourself and in turn, your body, your body will reflect that self-love...your perception will shift and you will begin to recognize your beauty. We are all beautiful. And if you continue to dwell on thoughts of love and appreciation and health - whatever that means to you - the universe will assist you with a match to that vibration.

"Nothing responds faster to your thoughts than your physical body."
~Abraham

Believe You Me

The universe, using the law of attraction, will always provide evidence to support our beliefs. But what are beliefs anyway? According to Abraham's teachings, our beliefs are just thoughts we keep thinking. And our beliefs, therefore, constitute the make-up of our reality.

Everything around us reflects our beliefs, because we are creating them, with our thoughts, as we go. And because the law of attraction is responding, we see evidence as proof of our beliefs. We may have been taught our beliefs by our parents, teachers, religious leaders, or friends, or we may have come to them on our own. But the cool thing is, we can change our beliefs if we wish to, simply by changing the thoughts we tell ourselves.

Which of your beliefs bring you comfort? Which do not? You can make a positive change in your life by focusing on those that bring you comfort, and letting go of those that do not.

What do you believe about your body, your appearance, yourself?
Do you believe you are beautiful? Strong? Healthy?
If not, it's time to change your thoughts. Dwelling on a reality that does not bring you joy will only reinforce your present state. Change your thoughts regarding your body, your looks, yourself, to reflect what it is that you want.

We are often so focused on what we don't like about ourselves, and then we wonder why it never changes or improves, no matter what we do (diet, work out, yada, yada). It's the *belief* regarding the thing we don't like about ourselves that causes us to be "stuck." Change your thoughts and your reality will change as well, effortlessly and permanently. When you change the way you feel about the way that you look, you will find that there is no reason to change the way you look, because you are beautiful and perfect as is.

Believe in your beauty.
Believe your body is healthy.
Believe that it feels good to feel good about yourself.

A belief is just a thought you keep telling yourself. Pay attention to your thoughts and steer the universe to assist you.

17/68

Wouldn't it be great to be able to see yourself in a beautiful light, always? Or most of the time, at least. We are a reflection of our feelings, so when you see the beauty in yourself, you see the beauty in others, and you see the beauty that is all around you.

You feel beauty full.

How many of us look into the mirror and see everything we don't like about our bodies? And how does it make you feel when you are focused on the things that you don't like?

Not great, to say the least.

What if you were to shift your focus from what you don't like to something you do like about your body? How would that make you feel?

Better? Most likely, even if for a moment.

And when you hold a thought/feeling for a mere 17 seconds, the law of attraction begins to respond. Maintain that good feeling for 68 seconds and your world has already started to shift. That's how quickly the universe responds to the vibration of our thoughts.

So pay attention to your thoughts, for goodness sake! Draw your attention away from what you do not want and direct it towards what you do want. It's that simple, but it does take practice. Pay attention to what feels good and stop living in a state of resistance. Use the laws of the universe to your advantage.

Imagination Appreciation

"'I am' is the creative force of the universe.
Whatever you attach 'I am' to you will become."
~Iyanla Vanzant

I am, is. Be conscious of your thoughts.

I am beautiful.
I am healthy.
I am abundant.
I am perfect health.
I am love.
I am energy.
You get the picture.

Wayne Dyer explained it by stating,
"You attract what you *are* rather than what you *want*."
So *be* whatever it is that you want to be. *Be* abundant
(feel abundance), and abundance will come. *Be*
healthy (feel healthy), and health will come. *Be*
beautiful (feel beautiful), and you are beautiful.

You have to begin to *feel it* before you can manifest or
experience it. So when I say "be abundant," I mean:
feel abundance to the point of believing it. It takes
practice and imagination, but when you achieve the
feeling, your vibration will affect your reality, which will
shift to reflect that feeling.

Remember how fun it was to "use your imagination" as
a kid? Many adults let their imaginations fade as they
get older. Responsibility takes over, and they begin to
"face reality."

Take time every day to turn away from reality
and tune in to your imagination. Using your imagination
is a powerful tool of deliberate creation, as achieving
the feeling of already having that which you desire,
leads to the vibrational alignment with the
manifestation of your desire.
As Abraham says, "don't face reality, create reality."

One of the best ways to tap into your imagination is by
writing down a vision of what you want.

"Imagination is the door through which disease as well as
healing enters. Disbelieve in the reality of sickness even
when you are ill;
an unrecognized visitor will flee!"
~Sri Yukteswar
(Yogananda's guru, from Autobiography of a Yogi)

Your Vision

You have to tell the story of how you want your life to look in order to create that life. If you stay focused on where you are, you'll stay exactly where you are.

Your imagination is your tool to create the reality of your desire. Conventional wisdom will teach you that "you have to face reality," but you really don't. (At least not every minute of every day!) Don't face reality if it doesn't feel good. Use your imagination to see life from a new perspective. Practice it daily, and things will begin to change. Of course, you can't spend all day every day day-dreaming. But the more time you devote to thoughts that make you feel good, the better you will feel, and the easier your life will become.

Within a year of being introduced to the law of attraction, I pinpointed my desire to be my own boss. I quit my part-time job in retail and started my own business, giving me the freedom of a flexible schedule and the opportunity to make more money while working fewer hours. With two young children at home, this was an enormous step in the right direction for the life *I* wanted to live. (I emphasize the "I" because this was *my* desire. Someone else may crave a full-time job. We all have unique desires.)

How did I accomplish this goal? By creating a vision and writing it down. These thoughts, created in my imagination and recorded in my journal, focused on a broad, general vision of working less, making more money, and being my own boss. I wrote daily, describing what I would do with my time and energy if I had more of it. Soon the vision became more detailed, and I realized that I could incorporate my years of retail experience and unique understanding of personal style into a business. I could help people to define their own sense of style, and in turn, help them feel good, which was necessary before they would feel that they looked good.

I've been in business for almost 10 years. On the surface, it would appear that my actions alone were the reason this shift in my life was made possible. But before I ever took action, I started with a vision. The vision triggered the vibration, which inspired the action, which lined up the circumstances (or cooperative components, as Abraham would call them), which led to the manifestation of the vision.

Super cool, right?

Take It Easy

As you begin to practice creating better feeling thoughts, be gentle with yourself. Years of telling yourself one thing and suddenly switching to another will be too big of a leap and will introduce resistance.

There is a lot of momentum behind old beliefs!

For instance, if you don't feel good about your body and you have a hard time believing "I am beautiful and healthy," that thought will cause resistance within you and will be counterproductive.

(That resistance would sound something like, "This is ridiculous. I feel fat, not healthy." Sound familiar?)

Instead, tell yourself that you're looking forward to feeling healthy. There is great power in subtly shifting the thought from "I feel fat" to "I am looking forward to feeling healthy." One comes from a state of hopelessness, the other hope.

When you commit to thinking thoughts that feel good, the universe will guide you into the reality you are creating for yourself, and it will feel effortless. For example, by focusing your thoughts on feeling better about yourself, you will start to make better choices at the subconscious level. You'll *want* to exercise. You'll *want* to eat healthier food. You'll *want* to drink more water. You won't have to *try* so hard to lose weight. Rather, it will happen naturally, *if that is what your body requires* (because maybe losing weight isn't necessary - remember that whole perception thing?).

You will be able to provide your body with whatever needs to feel (and ultimately be) healthy, without struggle. In every aspect of our lives, when we "replace effort and trying with relaxing and allowing," as Abraham teaches, reality begins to move in the direction of things we want. And remember, it won't happen overnight. Do your best to be patient and consistent, as things don't manifest instantly.

"India's unwritten law for the truth seeker is patience."
~Paramhansa Yogananda

Relief

One more time - this is really not about "thinking positively."
While thinking positively can't hurt, it's really about cultivating the thoughts that make you feel good, or feel relief.
It's about the way your thoughts make you *feel*.

The actual, tangible feeling in your body.
That feeling, or emotion, is what matters, because that's what evokes a response from the universe.

If "thinking positively" brings you to a good feeling place, fantastic. Go for it. But often, if we are feeling down, the idea of "thinking positively" feels almost impossible, or even makes us sick to our stomach. This is not the goal! Move in the direction of feeling better by choosing thoughts that bring you *relief*. The feeling of relief allows us to move up the "vibrational scale of emotions" that was referenced earlier. Finding thoughts that bring you relief will lead to feeling better, and the better it gets, the better it gets, because you are deliberately creating better feeling circumstances and allowing them to enter your life. That truth is universal law. Isn't it good to know?

Recognizing the choices we have with regards to our emotions will undoubtedly make this process of deliberate creation easier. I find Jill Bolte Taylor's scientific assessment of our body's reactions to our thoughts, given the circumstances we are confronted with, utterly fascinating:

In her chapter titled "Own Your Power" in <u>My Stroke of Insight</u>, Bolte Taylor states,

"Although there are certain limbic system (emotional) programs that can be triggered automatically, it takes less than 90 seconds for one of these programs to be triggered, surge through our body, and then be completely flushed out of our bloodstream. My anger response, for example, is a programmed response that can be set off automatically. Once triggered, the chemical released by my brain surges through my body and I have a physiological experience. Within 90 seconds from the initial trigger, the chemical component of my anger had completely dissipated from my blood and my automatic response is over. If, however, I remain angry after those 90 seconds have passed, then it is because I have chosen to let that circuit run."

90 seconds. It takes our bodies 90 seconds to process a negative emotion and release it. It is only our continued attention to the source of our anger that holds us in a place of feeling anger
(or sadness, or hurt, or frustration…).
Let it go, and feel relief within 90 seconds.
What a blessing, how our bodies are designed!
Let's take advantage of it.

Focus On What You Want

Abraham teaches us that every thought has two stories: what we want and the absence of what we want.

Focusing on what you want, as opposed to what you don't want, is the first step towards deliberately creating a new and improved reality. It is also the first step toward creating deeper, more natural beauty. Your new story is all about what you want. You don't have to "tell it like it is." Instead, tell it like you want it to be. Create a vision, and the vision will pull you forward. Write down what you see for your life assuming anything is possible. Anything. Write it down. Your finances, your body, your relationships, all of it - your whole life.
Create it.

"Without a vision, you're stuck in what you know. And the only thing you know is what you've already seen." ~Iyanla Vanzant

Often in our lives it is necessary to step away from reality and tell ourselves a "new" story. It's such a stretch for most people, because we've been taught since we were children the necessity to face reality in order to deal with any given situation. This simple lesson has led to the creation of more unwanted circumstances in our lives than possibly anything else. When you realize that your thoughts create your reality, you recognize the importance of the visions you hold in your mind. Holding yourself in a place of worry or fear will only bring things to worry and fear into your experience. On the other hand, creating a vision of what you want your life, or self, to look like, will only bring you closer to that reality. And the stronger you are able to feel the emotion of being in that place, that place where you want to be, the more quickly it will manifest into your life.

Seize the chance to tell a new story, starting right now! And remember that complaining will never serve you. Each time you think about, speak of, or write about things that are bothering you, the universe has no choice but to bring you more of that which you do not want.

Eliminating complaining can be one of the hardest, but most self-serving, shifts that a person can make. In <u>Women's Bodies, Women's Wisdom</u>, Christianne Northrup writes in her chapter "Steps for Creating Vibrant Health," "...women shoot themselves in the foot by complaining too much. It's a bad habit. Find friends who have the courage to consciously break it."

Unless you want the universe to deliver more things to complain about, do your best to not complain. Find something about the subject that is bothering you to appreciate, and give that feeling of appreciation your undivided attention. And if you cannot find anything about that subject to appreciate, then change the subject.

Do your best to not think about, to let go of things that don't feel good. It's possible. For real. I practice it every day. In our world today, there are a thousand ways to distract yourself from thinking about things that make you feel lousy. Use these tools to your advantage! Watch funny videos on YouTube for five minutes. Simple as that! Shift yourself from dwelling on something negative to watching something that makes you laugh. That's relief, and that's the ticket.

Complaining Is Dumb

As I mentioned, Robert and I have devoted much of our time to studying different teachers and aspects of spirituality. At one point, we spent a week at a yoga and meditation retreat. My intention with learning meditation in that setting was simply to begin a daily meditation practice, which I achieved. Many teachers of meditation will tell you to expect any number of shifts in your life once you begin to practice meditation regularly.

A few months into this new routine, I encountered one of these shifts. Robert came home from work (he's a veterinarian), and as was my daily ritual, I told him about my day. Or really, I told him about all the things that had driven me crazy throughout the day. My two-year-old, our financial struggles, friends, family, you name it, I complained about it. And on this particular day, only one thing changed - Robert stopped me. And he asked me to stop complaining. For good. He told me he no longer wanted to listen to me complain. Ever.

Honestly, I was blown away. I had hardly even realized that I'd been doing that (day after day, year after year - hard to imagine given all of the spiritual learning I had embraced to date, but true!) until he pointed it out and asked me to no longer use him as a source for venting my negative emotions, my daily frustrations. He just didn't want my negative energy turned in his direction anymore, even if it wasn't directed at him. And I could understand that. Yet I felt almost devastated by it. I felt that, as my husband, wasn't he expected to listen to me? How would I get these things off my chest, so to speak, if I didn't have him to dump it on to? I felt like I lost a part of my best friend. A major part. But I understood where he was coming from, so I did my best to honor his request. Instead of talking to him, I started writing my frustrations down in a journal. Only now I wasn't just writing about the trials and tribulations of my day, but about how awful I felt in general. And as I wrote, I felt worse and worse.

It didn't take me long to find myself at one of the lowest points in my life.
Enter Betsy, and subsequently, Abraham.

Let me give you a little background on the two of them. I first learned about Abraham after looking into the teachers behind the making of "The Secret." I checked out their website, and had even been receiving their daily inspirational emails for a couple of years. But until this moment in my life, I clearly hadn't really been ready to receive their message. So in a simple but incredibly powerful phone conversation when I was feeling so darn low, my dear friend Betsy re-introduced me to Abraham, at a time when I needed their guidance the most.

Betsy had discovered Abraham around the same time as my initial introduction to them, but took to their teachings immediately, like a fish to water. It came very naturally to her, and feeling good had been her dominant intention for as long as I had known her. The prior year to our conversation had been one of the most challenging in Betsy's life, to say the least. Her husband had succumbed to a brain tumor and died. He had been the love of her life, and no words can describe the level of grief she experienced with his loss. Yet, within one year, by focusing on thoughts that brought her relief, one day at a time, Betsy regained her deep love and appreciation for life, and her understanding of the importance of feeling good.

We were closely connected, in friendship and business, so we spoke to each other regularly. It was during one of these typical phone conversations that I confided in Betsy. I broke down and admitted to her how miserable I was feeling. I told her about how my kids were driving me crazy (they were 2 and 4 years old at the time), and my husband wouldn't listen to me complain about them or anything else for that matter. Her response caused another great shift in my life. Instead of agreeing with me and sympathizing with how hard my life was, and supporting my theory that Robert was being a huge asshole, she said, to paraphrase, "Good for him. No one should have to listen to this every day. Stop dwelling on everything that you feel is wrong with your life. You're only attracting more of the same. Start recognizing everything you have to appreciate."

I remember feeling almost stunned as I listened to her. But I knew immediately how right she was. When I told her that I'd been using a journal to record how lousy I felt, her response was along these lines: "Are you crazy?" She pointed out that the worst thing you can do, besides put a voice to your negative feelings, is to write them down. Journaling is a powerful creative tool, because it can activate strong emotions. So as I sat there each night, writing about how shitty I felt, that's the vibration I was generating. And I wondered why I wasn't feeling better!

Betsy's explanation was making perfect sense. Her crash course continued - every moment that I focused on feeling good, on allowing myself to have good feeling thoughts, I was attracting things to feel good about - abundance, health, happiness, etc. Whatever I wanted. When I dwelled on things that happened that I didn't appreciate, I got more of that. Keep in mind - this was coming from a woman who suffered one of the greatest losses that life could dole out. She was telling me that I had the power to turn this around, especially given the fact that my life was actually pretty fantastic and I had so much that I could focus on appreciating. She reminded me, "It feels good to feel good." It really does! So in that moment, that became my mantra. When my thoughts would slip into their old, negative patterns, I would catch myself and repeat, "It feels good to feel good!"

From that moment forward, my journals became filled with things that I love and appreciate about life. When you are feeling appreciation, you are feeling good. I have never written about something I don't like again, and I do my best not to give my negative feelings a voice. It's just not worth it.

The curveball: I have certainly found myself in the situation where it kind of feels good to not feel good. To feel sad, for instance. We don't have to beat ourselves up for not feeling good. It's ok. That's the thing. It's all ok, the good and the bad, because that's life. It's when we start to feel bad about *ourselves* that things get screwy, because you fall out of alignment with your inner being, who only feels love for you.

Be kind to yourself when you feel down. Some days are harder than others to feel happy, no doubt about that. But we *need* contrast in our lives. Contrast leads us to define what it is we want out of life. If your main intention, your dominant vibration, is to feel good, you'll soon see the contrast (whatever circumstance that's making you sad, or angry, or any negative emotion) and focus on the opposite of it. In other words, by looking at what you *don't* want, you can figure out what it is you *do* want.

What you want is just the opposite of what you don't want.

I don't want to feel stuck = I want to feel inspired.
I don't want war = I want peace.
I don't want to feel fat = I want to feel healthy.
I feel tired all the time = I want to have lots of energy.
I feel sad = I want to feel better.

Make the choice to believe that nothing is more important than that you feel good, and choose to be a deliberate creator of a beauty full life.

It Feels Good To Feel Good

So, what to do when you wake up on the wrong side of the bed, like I did the other day? Because god knows, when you start your day not feeling great, it's not very easy to think good feeling thoughts. And even the inspiration to want to feel good is tough to find.
But I knew it would feel better to feel better.

That day, I didn't feel like doing anything - not even getting out of bed to take a shower - so I stayed put. And as I hung out there for a bit (and meditated briefly), I realized that I could pretty much choose what to do that day, albeit the two appointments that I needed (and wanted) to keep. Such privilege. What a blessing, to have that kind of freedom. Appreciation washed over me.

Within a few moments of that wonderful feeling, I started to have inspired thoughts. Nothing monumental - just the basics, which is all I needed. I now felt like getting up and taking a shower, so I did. From there, on out, inspired thought was followed by inspired action.

Inspired thought followed by inspired action:
I (felt like going) went to the basement.

Inspired thought followed by inspired action:
I (felt like starting) started a load of laundry.

Inspired thought followed by inspired action:
I (felt like beginning) began the process of cleaning out my cluttered basement.

Inspired thought followed by inspired action:
I (felt like having) had something to eat.

Inspired thought followed by inspired action:
I (felt like writing) wrote this down.

Again, nothing monumental, just every-day stuff that needed to be done, but I felt like doing it, so I enjoyed the process. In turn, I could then feel good about all the things I had accomplished. These were things that I had been wanting to do, but hadn't realized that I wanted to do them when I woke up that morning, because it's hard to want to do anything when you feel lousy.

I appreciate knowing that there are simple steps that I can take – to inspire myself back into action. Some days are harder than others, but I find it's worth the effort to try.

Reminders

Ways that I pivot from feeling lousy to feeling better:

- Listen to music. (And sing along.)

- Watch something funny, i.e. a movie, a You-Tube clip, whatever

- Listen to an uplifting podcast

- Write in my journal about things I appreciate

- Call a good friend

- Take a bath

- Sleep

- Meditate

- Garden

- Color

- Go for a walk

- Do whatever it is that I *feel* like doing (not that I feel I *have* to do)

    Most importantly, I do my best to not beat myself up about anything I choose to do or feel, ever, good or bad. The greater, non-physical part of myself knows that I cannot do anything wrong and I will never get

it all done. My effort is to stay in alignment with that greater part of myself.
I remind myself regularly to listen to my inner guidance.
To let go of judgment.
To think thoughts that feel good.
To be ok with feeling bad.
Because wherever I am is exactly where I'm supposed to be.
It's all good. It really is.

Do Your Best

One of my all-time favorite books is <u>The Four Agreements</u>, by Don Miguel Ruiz. Four simple, powerful agreements to uplift yourself, and in turn, those around you.

The last of the agreements is "do your best," and while it's difficult to choose, I think it's my favorite. I have a feeling that you could make a drinking game out of the number of times I'll refer to that phrase throughout this work.

I do my best to think good feeling thoughts. I do my best to meditate daily. I do my best to eat consciously. I do my best to love myself. I do my best to let go of judgment.
In each and every moment of my life, I'm doing my best.

Do your best.
Nobody is perfect.
Abraham reminds us:
"You can never get it wrong, and you'll never get it done."
So just do your best.

STEP TWO

Meditate

Yogasta kuru karmati.
(Established in being, perform action.)

~Veda

Established in being, perform action.
Ancient words of wisdom.
What does this mean?

Ground yourself through meditation.
Spend time every day just being.
Not thinking, not doing, just being.
From this space, action will be effortless.
Ideas will flow.
Good feeling thoughts will be your normal.
Problems transform into solutions.
In meditation, you're connecting to pure consciousness,
the field of pure potentiality,
where all answers lie.

"As you gain more and more access to your true nature,
you will also spontaneously receive creative thoughts,
because the field of pure potentiality is also the field of infinite
creativity and pure knowledge."
~Deepak Chopra

Meditation is a gateway to connect with consciousness,
or who we really are. Our brains are always going to
be thinking thoughts - thoughts are good; they are
evidence that you are alive!
But the practice of meditation helps us to move to a
different level of thought, and sometimes, to no thought
at all. When we are in this state of mind, there ceases to
be resistance to our natural state of well-being.
Well-Being, consciousness, source energy; it's all the
same thing.

The most beneficial forms of meditation are methods
to relax the brain and release stress. When the brain
is allowed to reach subtler levels of thought, and
sometimes even no thought, all resistance to the
constant flow of Well-Being is released. As a result, the

activity following meditation is more effortless, efficient, and inspired.

Hence, yogasta kuru karmati.

I am. You are. Just be.

The Many Faces of Meditation

How to start? At the very least, set aside some time each day - even if it's just five minutes. Start by focusing on your breath. In his book <u>Perfect Health</u>, Deepak Chopra teaches an ancient practice, which relies on the mantra "so hum," meaning, "I am" in Sanskrit. When you breathe in, in your mind say "so" and when you breathe out, in your mind say "hum." Your focus on your breath and your attention to the words are enough to allow your mind to drift into a softer state of consciousness. This is a great technique to start with, because of its simplicity. It's also an easy meditation for children to learn, for the same reason.

It's not unusual to find this difficult at the beginning - most people do. That's why it's a practice! Over time, it becomes easier to sit still and allow your mind to relax. When you find that your thoughts have taken over and you're no longer thinking "so hum" or paying attention to your breath, simply begin again. Meditation is an ebb and flow between awareness to your practice and thinking thoughts. Eventually, the "thinking thoughts" part lessens and the "relaxing and allowing" part grows. This meditation is an example of how to use a mantra, with "so hum" acting as the mantra.

"A mantra is a mystical sound vibration encased in a syllable."
~George Harrison

Many meditation practices rely on a mantra to help quiet the mind. And thinking thoughts is a part of this process. Thoughts are just dust, which will eventually settle and lead to transcendence. Thoughts are a component of the release of stress, and again, they prove that we are alive. Don't be discouraged by them - having thoughts during meditation is completely normal and somewhat unavoidable. But there will come a time when the mind (or "dust") will settle, and eventually reach a state of "no mantra, no thought." For some, reaching this state happens quickly. For others, it takes years of practice. The moment may last for many minutes, or maybe just a second. It is in that moment of no thought that you release resistance.

There is no need to judge your meditations, as we are apt to judge everything in our lives. There is no such thing as a "bad meditation," no matter what happens. If you take five minutes to meditate and you feel that you were thinking thoughts for four minutes of it, that is just fine. Don't judge it. You did it, and that's all that matters. It's a practice. Regardless of what happens, when you meditate, you are doing your body and mind a service. Even if you don't feel it in the moment, what matters is how you feel after you meditate. More clarity, peace, connectedness, and effortlessness in your actions - those are the true benefits brought about by the release of stress and resistance to Well-Being.

I learned another great meditation practice from Eckhart Tolle. Quite simply, feel your hands. Not with your body, but with your mind. Place your hands in a comfortable position, close your eyes, and put your awareness on your hands. You may feel a slight vibration. You may feel the blood flowing to and from, the energy that lies within, allowing you to know (with your eyes closed) that your hands are, in fact, attached to your body.
Or, like me, you may feel nothing.

The first time I tried this, I found it surprisingly challenging. It seemed to me, when I sat quietly, closed my eyes, and tried to feel my hands, that I had no hands. I couldn't feel a gosh-darn thing. But still, it was a good exercise to practice, because I was drawing my attention away from my scattered thoughts and focusing it on my hands. This subtle shift of my awareness from whatever I was thinking, to paying attention to my hands, brought me into the present moment, which is all that really matters. Present moment awareness is so important, because at any given time, no matter what, all is well. Being present allows you to tap into the Well-Being that is our true nature, because you're not thinking (or worrying!) about anything other than what is happening right now.

There are literally hundreds of ways to meditate. Transcendental Meditation is another technique to quiet the mind and release stress. How does it translate into your daily life? Most find that the journey is the same, it's just a smoother ride. The bumps in the road are still there, but they are not jarring. You feel the bump as you ride over it, and continue on your way. That's on the deeper level. On a physical level, practicing TM is like plugging your body into a charger. It's energizing, and much better for you than a stimulant like caffeine. It's as good as a long nap without the groggy side effects. And you accomplish all of this in 20 minutes.

If you're willing and ready, you will absolutely find the time for a mediation practice. Use the time you might otherwise spend on Facebook, shopping online, watching television. If you make it a priority, it becomes a priority.
The choice is yours, as always.

All Is Well

So often we think that because of certain
circumstances in our lives, all is not well.
But that's not true. At every given moment, all is well.

Even if you are swamped in debt.
Even if you feel utterly overwhelmed.
Even if your marriage is falling apart.
The truth is, in this very moment in time, all is well.

If you live in the present moment, you are ok, you are
good, you are safe, you are intricately connected to
the energy that created the universe. You are allowing
it, or you are resisting it. Either way, all is well.

In his book Proof of Heaven, Eben Alexander explains
the three most important lessons he learned from his
powerful near-death experience:
One, you are loved and cherished.
Two, you have nothing to fear.
Three, there is nothing you can do wrong.

I think it's one of those wonderful "coincidences" in
life that one of the first things Alexander spoke upon
waking from his week-long coma and near-death
experience was "All is well." Which is the same phrase,
word for word, that Abraham uses regularly. It's pretty
much their tag line. Also, Alexander's description
of one of his most significant understandings of his
experience virtually matches another of Abraham's
most fundamental teachings:
"There is nothing you can do wrong." (Alexander)
"You can never get it wrong." (Abraham)
Simple truths being conveyed through interesting
avenues.

If you can remember this in those moments of feeling worry, anxiety, fear, and doubt, it can bring comfort and relief. That feeling of relief is what will bring you more relief. It's what is required to move you from where you are to where you want to be. Alexander reminds us that we all have access to the "idyllic realm" that he experienced. "We just forget that we do," he writes, "because during the brain-based, physical portion of our existence, our brain blocks out, or veils, that larger cosmic background, just as the sun's light blocks the stars from view each morning."

Meditation is one way, the easiest way, to connect to the non-physical part of ourselves, to return to the "idyllic realm." Whether you view this realm as the "larger cosmic background," or think of it simply as "heaven on earth," this unconditional source of love and well-being is one of which we are all a part and have the ability to experience.

"He who looks outside dreams, he who looks inside awakens."
~Karl Jung

Thank You, Nature

Meditation can take on hundreds of different forms. The important thing is to find which is right for you and practice it.

One of the most effortless forms of meditation is always just outside your front door - nature. Communing with nature is meditation, pure and simple. Taking the time to notice the intricate patterns on a leaf, the color and vastness of the sky, the texture of the bark on a tree, the ripples in a body of water, grains of sand, and on and on - nature is infinite and all around us, always.
One does not need to go on vacation or camp in the wilderness to find nature.
Step outside and look up.
Every neighborhood has a sky.

Sweet Dreams

Scientific studies have shown how meditation can improve sleep habits. Good sleep habits are another factor necessary to feel and look your best. When you sleep, resistance sleeps as well. And when you wake, you are, in essence, re-born. You've got a clean slate to start each and every day.

In the moment you wake, all is well. Your natural state of Well-Being is present at that moment. But resistance will set in quickly if you allow it to. It's our thoughts that quickly move us away from that natural state of Well-Being. Pay attention to how you feel immediately upon waking, and make it an intention to recognize the Well-Being that is there. Keep it there by paying attention to your thoughts. Try not to allow them wander into negative territory! Think about what you have to appreciate that day, starting with how good your covers feel. Won't that coffee taste delicious? Wouldn't it be nice if the sun shone today? Or maybe you'd prefer rain? Throw it out there. Just think about things that feel good to you before you even lift your head off of your pillow.
That will set you up for getting up "on the right side of the bed!"

The easiest way to begin this practice is to set the intention the night before to pay attention to the feeling of Well-Being that you feel when you first wake up, and think good feeling thoughts as you start your day. Also, it helps to make an effort to feel good as you go to sleep, because your point of attraction often picks up where you left off the night before. So again, notice how good your bed feels, how nice it is to be able to go to sleep, intend to have good-feeling

dreams, have sex, masturbate - do whatever you can
to feel good.
Just feel good as you go to sleep,
notice how good you feel upon waking,
and stick with that feeling throughout your day.

My Monkey

My own meditation practice has evolved through the years. My first attempts lasted all of 10 seconds - no exaggeration! From what I've always heard from other people, I suspect this is pretty typical, especially if you start on your own, without any formal guidance or training. In my case, I'd have the intention of "trying to meditate" for 10 minutes, sit down, close my eyes, my mind would absolutely race, list all the things that "needed to get done," and within 10 seconds, I'd give up, get up and get going.

Clearly, meditation didn't come easily to me at first. At that point in my life, I was much more concerned with doing than being. But since every single one of my teachers made it very clear that meditation was an essential element to connecting with the greater part of myself, I knew I had to keep trying.

I spent a couple of years investigating many different forms of meditation, including Deepak's "so hum" and Eckhart's "feel your hands," with Robert by my side. Eventually, we came to the conclusion that we would appreciate a more formal approach to establishing a daily practice - that is, we wanted to learn, from a teacher. (By the way, Robert had no problem feeling his hands. Harrumph.) At the time, we were pretty focused on Deepak Chopra's teachings, so we decided to attend a week-long seminar on yoga and meditation at the Chopra Center, where we would learn what they refer to as "Primordial Sound Meditation." I found the premise behind this particular type of meditation fascinating. Ancient sages had studied the different vibrations that occur throughout a 24-hour period during particular times of the year. Consider how everything feels and sounds at 3pm versus 3am, for instance, or at 3pm in December verses 3pm in May. There are different vibrations going on at each particular minute of every day! The sages attached a sound vibration, or mantra, to each of them, narrowing it to a total of 108 mantras. Your mantra is given to you based on the day and time of your birth.

Our main intention of committing to a meditation retreat was very clear - each of us wanted to begin a daily practice, as our meditations had thus far been sporadic. While I had known for some time the benefits of a daily practice, I hadn't yet been able to incorporate it into my life. I hoped that actually taking the time to be instructed, given a mantra, and immersed for a week would jump-start a true practice. And it did just that.

When we got home from the Chopra Center, we were definitely feeling invigorated and excited about our new commitment - meditate for 30 minutes twice a day - first thing in the morning (R.P.M. - Rise, Pee, Meditate) and in the evening. I was happy with the fact that we were able to work it into our schedules. I struggled with waking up earlier to fit it in, but made it happen. And my kids learned to play quietly when I meditated in the evening. (For the most part. This is where I really learned that "what happens in your meditation is part of your meditation.") There were certainly plenty of interruptions, but I learned to work around them, so to speak.

I have to admit, though, that while I came home feeling invigorated and excited, I also came home with what felt like a thousand unanswered questions. I was meditating daily, but I still wasn't feeling any sense of stillness within those meditations, and I wasn't sure if that was normal. My type-A-ness was wreaking havoc - monkey brain plus frustration over not being able to quiet the monkey brain equaled more frustration. I longed for a teacher, someone who could answer my many questions and help set my mind at ease. Enter: Transcendental Meditation.*

Transcendental Meditation, a practice to quiet the mind and release stress, was brought to the West by Maharishi Mahesh Yogi in the late 1960's. I first learned about it soon after leaving the Chopra Center - with all of my unanswered questions, I was searching for answers. I read Chopra's autobiographical Return of the Rishi, and discovered that Deepak was taught TM by the Maharishi when he first came to the United States. I wondered how it differed from Primordial Sound Meditation, and whether it would be worth learning. A part of me knew that the answer to that question was a definitive yes, but not yet. Timing is everything, as they say, and sometimes it's best to wait until the timing is right. So I put the idea on the back burner and let it brew.

A lot happened between learning about TM and learning TM, most notably, my reintroduction to the teachings of Abraham. Robert made the observation, and I whole-heartedly agree, that their message may not have resonated with us so deeply had we not been meditating - and connecting to pure consciousness, to the infinite field of intelligence - so regularly in the months leading up to that moment. It seemed that despite my occasional worry that my meditation practice "wasn't doing me any good," my practice had been affecting me on levels that I wasn't always consciously aware of. (Before I learned better, I was always more concerned with how I felt *during* meditation, failing to recognize the improvement that

I felt in my life *outside* of meditation.) Our practice opened and allowed connections that we didn't know existed, and continues to do so to this day.

Eventually, when the time was right, my path led me back to TM. (Truth be told, it was another Oprah Winfrey show that brought my focus back to that long ago desire to learn TM.) I reached out to the TM teacher in my area and knew immediately that it was the right time to learn this practice. I have found that not only do I appreciate TM's fundamental emphasis of effortlessness, but also the hundreds of scientific studies devoted to TM, and therefore the well-documented scientific evidence of the many, many benefits to our physical bodies that a TM practice brings. I also appreciate the lifelong connection to a teacher and global community of teachers and fellow practitioners. I have many people to reach out to when I have a question, and that, for me, is a beautiful thing.

Of course, I also know that the answers to all of our questions are inside each and every one of us. Infinite intelligence is who we really are, and meditation connects us to that powerful Source Energy.

*For more information on Transcendental Meditation, visit tm.org and watch the introductory video.

Listen

Meditation is a space where there are no goals, no expectations, no judgments.
Meditation shifts you into present moment awareness.
It connects you to the Source Energy that is our true essence.
It moves you beyond your ego.
It transfers you from left-brain thinking to right-brain awareness.
It releases resistance and connects you to the ever-flowing state of Well-Being that is at our core.

"When you pray, you talk to God; when you meditate, you listen."
~Diana Robinson

Kindred Spirits

The first time I had the pleasure of seeing a real, live sloth was at the zoo in Naples, Florida. I could not believe how cool this guy was, how incredibly slow his movements were from one point to another. Seriously, it's hard to describe - sloths move REALLY slowly. It was love at first sight.

I continue to be amazed by these special animals, and was fortunate enough to have had the opportunity to witness them in their natural habitat while visiting Nicaragua. On our "Sloth Quest," (yes, we went on a sloth quest and it was awesome) I figured out a few things that makes it easier to understand why I find them so damn cool.

Sloths are not lazy, as humans often perceive them. They are just slow. They like to take it easy. They are so chill, in fact, that the two-toed sloths living in Nicaragua have no natural predators. On average, they live to be 50 years old. Let me say that again - they have no natural predators and live to be 50. How amazing is that? It's not often that you hear those statistics concerning animals who live in the wild.

I want to learn from the sloth - to slow down, take it easy, chill out and reach a state of mind where you're so relaxed and at ease, no one bothers to fuck with you.

Inspired Action

When I think about my life before meditation, and the almost constant feeling of "having to get things done," I have to acknowledge the blessing it has been to understand what it means when Abraham teaches us, that "you'll never get it done and you'll never get it wrong."

The first part - "you'll never get it done" - has been one of my most powerful lessons. I relayed this lesson to a friend of mine once when she was feeling overwhelmed with her never-ending list of to-do's. And that's just the point - they are never-ending. What a beautiful thing to make peace with and accept that fact. She thought it over for a moment or two, and as it sank in she said, "I guess so. I mean, what happens when you get it all done?" And I replied, "You die." We had a good laugh, but it's really true.

You never get it all done; you're not supposed to. Life is a series of things to do, spurred by our desires. Whether it's laundry or dishes or starting a business or creating art or going on vacation, there is always something to do, and we will never get it all done. So relax and enjoy the journey, as so many people have encouraged us to do, and do things when you feel inspired to do them, rather than when you feel you have to. Whatever it is that you would like to accomplish will feel much better if there is inspiration, rather than obligation, behind it. Which leads us right back to where we started: "established in being, perform action."

Deepak Chopra once said, "We are human beings, not human doings."
It really is important to just "be" sometimes.
And that's meditation.

STEP THREE

Breathe Deeply

Breath is life force flowing through you.

~Abraham

A deep breath can be the segue between a bad feeling thought and a good feeling thought, or a feeling of relief.
A deep breath can be a reminder to be in the present moment.
A deep breath can rid the body of toxins.
A deep breath can help pivot your thoughts from one direction to another.
A deep breath is a pause.

As we go through our day-to-day lives, we are often acting on autopilot. The focus and awareness that we could bring to our actions, ceases to exist. Knee-jerk reactions to things that take place around us become commonplace. Someone says something that hits a nerve, and we react. But what if there was a brief pause before we reacted? What if, in that pause, we realized our reaction would benefit no one? Wouldn't it be better not to react, to instead channel that energy in another direction? How many unnecessary confrontations could we avoid by that redirection of energy? A regular meditation practice, and an awareness of breath, cultivates this pause. Over time, the pauses add up, and things that might have once bothered you no longer do. We're able to maintain feeling good for longer and longer periods, without dwelling on negative emotions. Our lives become noticeably better.

I love Eckart Tolle's use of a symbol for pause in his book, The Power of Now. In fact, I love it so much that I had the symbol tattooed on my wrist as a reminder. Every now and then, in the midst of some sort of chaos, Robert will walk up to me and press it. Literally, he presses the pause button on my wrist. Not only do I pause, but I also usually laugh.
And I take a deep breath.
And I feel better.

When you are confronted with something unpleasant, rather than having a knee-jerk reaction and allowing your thoughts to spiral in a negative direction, automatically reacting to the conditions, the mere act of pausing to take a breath can have a powerful effect on your vibration.
It's calming.
It's centering.
It can help propel your thoughts, and in turn, your vibration, in a positive direction.
On the other hand, if you allow yourself to sink into negative feeling thoughts, you will stay in the feeling of negativity, or begin to feel even worse.

Which direction would you prefer, if you knew that you had the choice? Having the ability to pause, breathe deeply, and choose to let go of anger, frustration, any negative emotion as quickly as it comes is a blessing for anyone who chooses to cultivate it.

Every Little Thing's Gonna Be Alright

~Bob Marley

For many of us, worrying is second nature - people do it all the time. Unfortunately, worrying can have harmful side effects when you consider that your thoughts create your reality. As Abraham likes to say, "Worrying is using your imagination to create what you do not want." Fortunately, it's easy enough to avoid once you begin to pay attention. Start to recognize when you are worrying. It often starts small. A single worried thought creeps in, and our nature is to expand upon it, assisted by the law of attraction responding to your vibration. The longer you think thoughts of this kind, the more prevalent they will be in your life.

Instead, I would encourage you to end habitual worrying, and one way do so is by taking a deep breath when worried thoughts arise. Simple as it seems, by redirecting your focus from your negative thought to your breath, you've begun the process of letting go, both of the thought, and more importantly, the feeling that comes with the thought. (Who needs that nasty feeling in the pit of your stomach, ever, right?) Not only does taking a deep breath change your focus, it also feels good, so you are replacing the yucky worried feeling with the cleansing feeling associated with a deep breath. Now is your chance to move forward, to move to a better feeling thought!

4 Steps to End Habitual Worrying:

1) The worried thought comes, you recognize it.
2) You take a deep breath.

3) The worried thought and feeling are released and replaced with the cleansing breath.
4) You pivot your thought to something that feels better.

With practice, this becomes second nature, and you find yourself worrying less and less.
Because what is there to worry about, really, once you *know* that all is well?

When I was the mother of two young children, I often worried for their well-being. I played out scenarios in my head where they were injured, or even killed. At a certain point, I started to recognize how these thoughts made me feel (awful) and what effect they might be having on my vibration (this is when I had just begun my awakening regarding our vibrational nature). I quickly realized, *decided* really, that I needed to stop this habitual worrying. I did my best to replace any thought of my children being harmed with the following mantra: I am grateful that my kids are alive, healthy, and full of joy, which I would then follow with a deep, cleansing breath.

Now I look back on that time and realize that I can't even remember when all the worry ended. But it did - the worry habit was broken. And while I do still have the occasional worried thought, I prefer to quickly notice the worry, and let it go. No reason to dwell in that thought and create a story that has not actually happened that feels like shit. It's shocking when you think about how often we do that.
No thank you!

Trust and Faith

I once asked an aryuvedic doctor, "What's the opposite of worry?"
To which she replied, "Trust and faith."

Trust and faith - the opposite of worry.
Consider that for a moment.
Consider the possibility that anytime you have a worried thought, you replace it with a deep breath and the words "trust and faith."

Trust and faith in the universe, that everything will be ok, that everything is always ok, that everything is always working out for you. There is no reason to worry. There is nothing to fear.

Do your best not to worry about things. Your health, politics, your children, your parents, the environment, your retirement, your kids' college fund, your finances. Life offers us a slew of things that we could worry about. But worries are thoughts, and you can choose your thoughts. What if you had trust and faith that everything would always work out?
What if that became your mantra?

Everything is always working out for me.

Perhaps life would reflect that belief.

Fun Things To Think

All is well.
There are no shortages.

Everything is always working out for me.

It feels good to feel good.

Adventure without risk.

There is great love here for you.

You can never get it wrong and you'll never get it done.

I am never early; I am never late. I am always on time.

Embrace uncertainty.

Let go of effort and trying and replace it with relaxing
and allowing.

Spark joy.

It's always easy to find rock star parking.

Ease.

A belief is just a thought you keep thinking.

Life is full of green lights and green arrows.

Worrying is using your imagination to create what you
don't want.

There is nothing to fear.

Do your best.

(Acknowledgments: Abraham, Marie Kondo, Eben
Alexander, Robert, Source)

It's Elemental

Argon.
A character from Lord of the Rings? Not so much. I practically failed high school chemistry, so I had never heard of Argon until fairly recently, while watching Tom Shadrach's film, "I Am." So here's the deal - I'm no expert, but this is my understanding of the beauty of Argon...

Argon is one of the seven noble gases, an element found in the earth's atmosphere. It constitutes 1% of the air that we breathe, and it has always been here and it will always be here. It connects us to past and future generations, in that the Argon that was breathed in and out by, say, Jesus, for instance, is the same Argon that we are breathing in and out today. It is the same element that future generations will be breathing in and out.
It's almost as if it transcends space and time, and binds all of humanity together.
We are all connected.
We are all one.

Pivot

Here's an example of a thought process that I used one day, where I incorporated deep breaths as a means to relax and pivot my thoughts towards enjoying the journey, no matter what:

First day of school. We pick the kids up and head to their favorite place for "froyo." (That's frozen yogurt, for those of you unfamiliar with teenage vernacular.) Delicious treat, and back to the car. Turn the key in the ignition - engine turns over but does not start. Initial reaction? Minor panic, due to thoughts triggered instinctually at this point.

How much will this cost to fix?
Will we need a new car?
How would we pay for that?
What are we going to do?

This all happens within five seconds. Stop. Deep breath. Pause. Notice that those thoughts, leading to those feelings, will not serve me in this moment, or ever. Ten, maybe fifteen seconds have passed since the car would not start. Deep breath. Everything is ok. We are fine. We are close to home. Let's walk home and begin to find a solution.
As many wise teachers will tell you, you solve a problem when you focus on the solution, not the problem.

Deep breath. Decide to call AAA while walking home. This does not need to feel like a big deal. It is not a big deal. Feel a sense of well-being. An understanding that all is well. Deep breath.

My call to AAA is not going through. Try again. Another disconnection. Try two more times, without reaching anyone. Not upsetting. Realize that it's time to stop trying, and wait until we get home to call again.

Breathe. Enjoy our walk. Enjoy walking and talking with Harper, our youngest daughter. And Lola, her big sister. And Robert. My family. There is so much to appreciate about this moment. All is well. This is not a big deal. Everything is going to work out just fine.

One block from home, we pass a tow truck parked on the street with a phone number painted on the side. Robert and I exchange a glance, a smile. Call the number, leave a message. Finish our walk home. Begin to place another call to AAA when Robert's phone rings - the local tow truck returning our call. He's willing to tow the car across town to our mechanic right now, and it won't cost much. He'll meet us immediately. Robert heads back to the car. Calls me five minutes later. Tow truck driver got the car started, and charges us nothing. We can drive it to our mechanic. Which we do. Mechanic runs codes and finds nothing obviously wrong. He is able to start the car multiple times without a problem. I mention that our headlight is out, can he fix it? He does. $40 and done.

Other than the initial five seconds, I felt entirely fine, comfortable, even a sense of fun. There was a time when the story would not have unfolded in such a manner. There was a time when the car not starting would have sent me into an utter panic, a feeling of overwhelment, even despair, over having to deal with the situation at hand. Instead, I enjoyed the ride to and from our mechanic (30 minutes each way), catching up on podcasts and feeling relaxed. Our headlight was

fixed, which needed to be taken care of. Everything worked out perfectly.
Deep breath.

Ok, full disclosure here: I did have to take my car back in and it did need some repairs. But it was ok. I wasn't upset about it, because I choose to believe that it's all ok, always. The good, the bad and the ugly.
It's as it's supposed to be.
It's as we have created it.
We come into our physical experience, where the greater part of ourselves is non-physical, knowing what we're in for. We are given what we've asked for before coming to have this physical experience.
The contrast we experience in our lifetimes fuel our desires, and in turn, our expansion.
So, it's all ok.

Like Robert says,
"It's about enjoying the journey, no matter what turn it takes."

Find peace with whatever happens in your life.
That's the work, the effort.
Find peace.

Deep breath.

STEP FOUR

Nourish Yourself

"There is benefit in <u>everything</u> that you eat."

~Abraham

The energy that we put into our body matters. When you consider our energetic make-up at a molecular level, the phrase "you are what you eat" rings very true. If you choose to eat meat, for example, would you rather consume an animal who lived comfortably, was able to live in its natural state, eating what it naturally eats, and had access to fresh air and sunshine, or an animal who was confined to a crate, was fed food that wasn't compatible to its digestive system, and therefore had to be fed antibiotics in order to maintain its poor health before it was slaughtered for your consumption? The energy of whatever you're consuming matters to your health and life. Eating consciously is one part of nourishing yourself.

Water is another component to nourishing yourself. It is the ultimate purifier. It hydrates our bodies, it detoxifies our bodies, and flushes unnecessary matter (like excess fat and toxins) from our bodies. On average, water constitutes over half of our body's make-up. Drinking half of your body weight in ounces each day is extremely beneficial to our physical bodies.

But most of all, nourishing yourself is about paying attention to how you think about what you consume. Your thoughts have a significant affect on how you feel and look. We all know, in this diet obsessed culture, what is good for us and what isn't, for the most part. Fruits and vegetable are "good." Partially hydrogenated oils are "bad." But how do our beliefs affect how these "good" and "bad" foods influence our bodies? And why do we feel the need to judge food as good or bad in the first place?
What is good is feeling good. That's what matters. The most important component to nourishing yourself is feeling good about whatever you consume.

Here's the thing...when you hold the intention that nothing is more important than feeling good, you will inherently *want* to nourish your body with healthy foods and water. You won't have to *try* - trying introduces resistance, which does not feel good. You will *want* to, because you will be in a state of allowing Well-Being to flow through you, and you will be inspired to nourish yourself. You will eat what you want, and even foods deemed unhealthy can be good for you in this state of mind. The worst thing you can do is eat or drink something that you *think* or *believe* is bad for you, as then it will be. Your cells have the ability to receive nourishment from the foods you eat and eliminate the rest if you allow them to, but we block this ability with our thoughts. If, when you're eating something, you're thinking, "I should not be eating this. This is really bad for me. I feel bad about myself, because I'm eating this food," you are literally blocking your cells' ability to do their work. Serious self-sabotage.

Instead, believe in your body's ability to maintain health. Have the intention of being healthy. You really won't want to eat large amounts of "unhealthy" food. You really will want to eat more healthy foods and drink sufficient amounts of water. Your intention will be driving your action. The key is maintaining the intention, because in that space, connected to Source, you will naturally make healthy choices more frequently. An 80/20 balance feels good to me, so I know that if I'm making healthy choices 80% of the time, I don't feel bad about the 20% of the time that I choose to eat or drink something that doesn't constitute "healthy" nourishment. Feel good no matter what, and it will be good for you.

Nothing is more important than that you feel good!

Good Food

Feel good about the food that you eat.
Abraham tells a story of Esther having dinner with
an attractive, tall, slender woman, who ordered
appetizers, two entrees, and dessert and ate it all.
At the end of the meal, Esther joked,
"You realize we can no longer hang out."
To which her friend replied, "Well, food is my friend."

How many of us view food as our friend? I've
encountered far more people who believe food is their
enemy. When you don't feel good about the food
you put into your body, how could that food possibly
be good for you? No matter what it is! Everything you
eat is a benefit to you. Again, the most important part
of nourishing yourself is paying attention to how you
feel about what you are eating. Make friends with it,
whether it's a green smoothie or a chocolate chip
cookie.
Appreciate both.

What You Resist Persists

In our vibrational universe, Well-Being is all there is. Whenever you are feeling negative emotion, you are experiencing a resistance to the flow of Well-Being energy. There is no opposite force - no negative energy- there is only Well-Being and resistance to it.

Most of us are unaware of this internal resistance. We are so accustomed to the negative thoughts produced by our ego, regarding our bodies, our intellect, our relationships, our circumstances in general, that we barely even notice the ongoing negative banter. Anytime you are thinking thoughts that make you feel angry, frustrated, hopeless, sad, etc., you are experiencing resistance to Well-Being, because you are experiencing a disconnect between your greater, non-physical self which IS Well-Being.

Recognition of any resistance is necessary to improve your point of attraction, as resistance will only perpetuate more resistance - hence, what you resist persists. Given the fact that your resistant thoughts are often fairly sub-conscious, in that they come and go and come and go and you are barely aware of them, the practice of meditation is extremely beneficial to release resistance. When you meditate, not only do you shift your perspective away from these thoughts, you ideally direct your mind to a quiet space, silence even, where there is no resistance, because there is no thought at all. But you can also make the effort to release resistance outside of meditation, by *appreciating*.

Remember that feelings of love, joy, happiness, hopefulness, and appreciation signal your connection to Well-Being, because these feelings are in alignment with who you really are.

What You Focus On Grows

Along the same lines, pay attention to the fact that *what you focus on grows*, whether it is positive or negative. This is why it's important to look at things from a positive perspective, or a place of appreciation. The universe doesn't see positive and negative, it only feels the difference between the positive feeling and the negative feeling, and responds accordingly, drawing to you more of whatever you are feeling.
If you want to feel good about your body, find something that you *like* about it and focus on it.

That's a challenge for some, and I invite you to accept it.
Find something you like about your body and focus on it.

When I first started this practice, I realized that every time I looked in the mirror, like a falcon eyeing it's prey, my eyes would zero in on my belly. In reality, there is nothing wrong with my belly. But in my mind, I didn't like it. Sure, I could tell myself that it's fine, there's nothing wrong with it, that it's a perfectly normal belly, but truthfully, I still wouldn't like it, and looking at it in the mirror inevitably would not feel good. So I stopped looking at it! I looked at my legs, or my hair, or my eyes instead, all of which I can appreciate. I can look at my legs and feel good. I can look at my hair and feel good. I can look at my eyes and feel good.
So why not look at what feels good, and not pay attention to what doesn't? It just feels better to focus on something that feels good, whether you're talking about your body or anything else in your life.

And remember - conversely, if you choose (yes, choose) to focus on (and complain about) things that aren't working out for you, that you feel bad about, the universe has no choice but to deliver more of the same, because what you focus on grows.
Feel good and good will come.

He Who Shall Not Be Named

No, I'm not talking about Lord Voldemort.
I'm referring to a certain person in our political
atmosphere at the moment who, I believe, has been
given entirely too much attention. As a result, his
influence has grown. The situation perfectly exemplifies
the idea that what you resist persists and what you
focus on grows. So many people have made it their
choice to actively resist this man. He has been lavished
with our attention. I was watching a late night talk show
whose host had clear disdain for this individual, and
throughout the course of the show, he mentioned him
by name at least 15 times.
That's a lot of focus.
A lot of resistance.
A lot of attention to a subject that conjures so many
negative emotions from so many people, adding that
energy to our our collective consciousness.

I wonder what might be different right now had we not
honored him with our attention.
Had the media and all the individuals on social media
not taken action when they felt the strong negative
emotions fueled by his rhetoric.
Had we all just ignored him, and focused on a
candidate who made us feel good instead of awful.
Where would he be now? Where would we be?
I wonder.

Give things you want in your life the benefit of your attention.
Do your best to focus on what you want, and watch it grow.

"Far too many people are looking for the right person, instead of trying to be the right person."
~Gloria Steinem

Your Boobs Look Fantastic

Recently I had the pleasure of working with a woman who (also) had an issue with her belly. She thought it was too big. As her personal stylist, it was my job to ensure that she felt good in all of her clothes. If she tried something on that, from my objective perspective, looked great, I told her, "Your boobs look fantastic." She liked her boobs, so it was easy for her to believe me.

My goal was to shift her focus from her belly (because we all inevitably pay too much attention to the one thing - or more than one - that we don't like about our bodies) and move it to her boobs, since they were a feature on her body she could appreciate.

We can all do this. Focus on what feels good. It doesn't matter if you're a size 2 or 24 - we all have parts of our bodies that we don't appreciate. The goal is to find and focus on things we *do* appreciate. Bugged by your belly? thighs? hips? legs? ankles? whatever??? Find something that you *like* about your body - lips, feet, hands, shoulders, hair, boobs, whatever. Focus on that instead. The more you find to appreciate, the better.

When I tell myself that "my boobs look fantastic," (instead of the old, "ugh, that belly") I'm releasing resistance and allowing thoughts and feelings that manifest health and balance.

Tune in to your natural state of being – perfect health.

Eat Consciously

I'm sure the phrase "eat consciously" means a lot of different things to different people.
Here's what it means to me:

- I shop primarily at our local organic co-op.

- I feel really good about the food I buy there. It feels good to me to know that the food I'm eating and feeding my family has not been sprayed with chemicals and often comes from a local farmer.

- I buy grass-fed beef whenever possible. It feels good to me to know that the animal I'm consuming was able to eat food that it was designed to eat, and that it lived in it's natural state, with space, fresh air and sunshine.

- I am willing to pay a higher price for quality meats, and in turn, eat less of it. My family eats a meat-centered meal, on average, 2-3 times a week.

- There are more whole foods than processed foods in my pantry and refrigerator. So, I have more ingredients for things, rather than boxes or jars of pre-made food. If I make spaghetti for dinner, for instance, I make the sauce instead of using a jar of sauce. (Spaghetti sauce: olive oil, chopped onion, garlic, 28oz. fresh or canned diced tomatoes, basil (optional), extra veggies (optional), meat (optional), Italian seasonings. Easy breezy, and not very time consuming.)

- I utilize the bulk section of my grocery store whenever possible for basics such as rice, beans, grains, nuts and spices.

- I love my rice-cooker, my blender, my juicer, and my food processor. They are all helpful tools.

- I drink lots of water. I do my best to start my days with 32oz. of warm lemon water, which I learned from participating in "The Conscious Cleanse" a couple of years ago. When this particular cleanse was introduced to me by a friend who is a physician, I intuitively knew it would be right for me. Given it's name, it clearly aligned with my own beliefs, and as soon as I began to read the corresponding book written by Jo and Jules, the creators of this cleanse, I knew I was right. I learned a lot from them. (http://consciouscleanse.com)

- For the most part, I eat either sprouted or sourdough bread. Sprouted grains, as well as sourdough, have much greater health benefits than any other kind of bread. In fact, most of our bodies recognize sprouted grains as a vegetable instead of a starch. (For more information, see https://www.culturedfoodlife.com/sourdough-sprouted/)

- I almost always use organic coconut, grapeseed or sesame oil to cook with, as these oils maintain their molecular integrity at high heat, unlike olive oil. I love olive oil, but prefer to use it raw, such as in salad dressings.

- I rarely use the microwave. According to the Ayurvedic philosophy, any reheating of meals reduces the vitality of the food. Using a microwave to reheat food is the equivalent of moving from fresh squeezed orange juice to Tang.

- I do my best to eat at least 2 portions of organic greens every day, because I know that when I do, my body appreciates it. My friend Monica pointed out that the whites of my eyes get brighter when I eat ample greens. I like that.

- Often at least one of these portions are in the form of a green smoothie or fresh juice. I learned a ton of fantastic green smoothie recipes from "The Conscious Cleanse," (http://consciouscleanse.com/book/) and I stick with a favorite juice that I first had at Urban Beets, a great juice bar in Milwaukee, consisting of pear, collard greens, cucumber, orange, and lemon.

- I do my best to feel good about everything I eat, no matter what. I read this on Facebook the other day and thought, "Well that just about sums it up!"

"Eat real food that makes you feel alive and makes you want to do things that make you feel alive. Donuts aren't capable of doing that. However, if you enjoy them every once in awhile, and then say, 'That was nice, and now I am done with you,' donuts are wonderful. The size of your thighs (or any other body part) is not what matters in this one life we have. What matters is how we feel when we are here and how we make others feel. Focus on that." (http://www. scarymommy.com/want-my-daughter-know-as-grows-up/)

Right on, sister.

Eating consciously evolves over time. I took my time making these changes and incorporating them into my life. There's no rush to this, to any of it. It's simply paying attention. It's being aware, and being conscious of an intention to feel good. As Abraham says, "be easy with yourself."

Have fun with it, with everything. It's what we're here to do.

Save The Worst For Last

I used to have a habit of eating until I was so full that I felt sick. When I finally realized that this was a habit I could change, something clicked. I was always saving the best for last. If there were three pieces of pizza/fish/ bites of pie/fill in the blank, I would eat the first two and then be completely full, but still feel the need to eat the last piece because it was the best, and I'd been saving it, dammit!

I finally understood how convoluted that approach was.

Always eat the best first.

Saving the best for last with your food is counterproductive.

It encourages you to eat after you're already full.

[Burp]

A Note About Eating Consciously

I think it's worth noting that these practices were not something that came naturally to me, until I put my focus on wanting to attain as close to "perfect health" as possible. (I'm sure I was originally inspired by that phrase when reading Deepak Chopra's book by that name, Perfect Health.) At the time, my favorite thing to eat for lunch, which I did almost daily, was a bagel with butter, salami and cheese. I also loved Coke and Doritos. Does that give you a window into my psyche concerning food? If not, I can go on. Let's just say that I liked to joke that I had the taste buds of a five year old - processed mac and cheese and frozen pizza were at the top of my list of favorite foods. (Full disclosure: pizza, of any sort, is still at the top of that list.)

I point this out because I think it's fun to realize that anyone can adapt to eating consciously, if I can. And I feel so much better for having done so. I still, on occasion, indulge in some of my old vices (vices go hand-in-hand - you can assume that if I'm nursing a hangover, I'm eating Doritos and drinking a Coke), but I now know that:

a) They need not be considered vices, because everything you eat is good for you when you're in the right state of mind.

and

b) By making feeling good a priority in my life, I much prefer more nourishing, whole foods to any of my old cravings.

Your thoughts surrounding your body and how you view yourself will affect how you eat, and how your food will affect your body. If you see yourself in a good light - I am healthy, I am strong - the law of attraction will draw those circumstances to you. The choices you make regarding food will naturally, effortlessly, be healthy. You won't have to "diet," because your daily choices will nourish your body. You won't have to abandon the foods that don't necessarily nourish you. Instead, you'll find that you only want to eat them in moderation, and they will all be a benefit to you.

The universe will guide you if you allow it, and you allow it by being aware of your thoughts.

Nourish yourself. Love yourself. It's that simple.

Release Resistance

Body image is a topic that sparks a ton of resistance, especially for American women. So much so that it's one of the many things we refer to as a *"battle"* or a *"struggle."* (Disease would be another. "She's *fighting* cancer.") Very resistant words, and more importantly, feelings associated with them.

You may have noticed that I used the words "feeling fat" in Step 1, because I have felt that way and I have told myself that story far too many times throughout my life, and I don't believe I'm alone in that. Interestingly, I've received a lot of flack for the use of that one particular word. People have suggested that I change the line to, "I feel weak," or "I feel unhealthy." But the truth is, when I'm in a certain state of mind and I look in the mirror, I feel "fat." I don't feel weak. I don't feel unhealthy. I feel fat. That's what I tell myself, because that's what I feel. What's interesting is that we perceive "fat" as a bad word. Other cultures don't have the same reaction that we have when it comes to that word, because being fat in other cultures is not a big deal. When they see a fat person, they're not afraid to say, "It's right there, next to that fat person." But we've attached this horrible stigma to it - like someone who is fat should be ashamed, and not acknowledged. There is no shame in being fat. Fat people are beautiful. All people are beautiful. Let's not equate "fat" with "shame." It's not a bad word. It's not a bad anything. If you're fat and happy, fantastic. The goal isn't to be thin. The goal is to be happy.

That said, if you're feeling negatively about your body, whether it's "I'm too fat" or "I'm too thin" or "I'm too this" or "I'm too that," it benefits you to release resistance as much as possible. You take your body everywhere you go (or really, it takes you), which is why we think about it so much. I've found that if I can catch myself in the negative story-telling about my body, and then do my best to shift to a better feeling thought, I can almost feel the vibrational shift. I soon feel encouraged to care for my body, with exercise, nourishing food, better sleep, etc. My focus, my effort, is to let go of resistance around the subject of my body.

Fortunately, my dominant vibration has generally been that of a healthy body. I've always believed that about myself, despite my occasional negative brain chatter. If your experience is different, and you've *struggled* with weight for most of your life, and have made food your *enemy*, it is all the more necessary to begin to let go of the resistance holding you away from your natural state of being: perfect health.

Love yourself. No matter what the scale says. Appreciate your body. Find something to focus on and pay attention to it, rather than dwelling on what you don't like. Be kind to your body! Nourish it with good feeling thoughts, which will lead you to nourish it with good feeling food and good feeling choices. Transformation begins from within. When you make feeling good your dominant intention, everything else will fall into place.

STEP FIVE

Recognize Your Worthiness

Love who you are.

~Anonymous

Synonyms for the word worthy:
deserving, good, important.
Antonyms for the word worthy:
no-good, undeserving, valueless, worthless.
Which feels better?

Each and every human being comes from and is directly connected to a boundless energy source that is only, ever, always worthy. No one is truly an antonym to worthy except in their own minds. If those negative thoughts plague you, you can change the way you feel about yourself by beginning to recognize your inherent worthiness.

We are all worthy.
We are worthy of love.
We are worthy of abundance.
We are worthy of beauty.
We are worthy of living our lives as we want them to be.
We are worthy of friends who are kind.
We are worthy of healthy, loving, intimate relationships.
We are worthy of a good education.
We are worthy of anything and everything that we desire.

You can only really achieve true beauty when you begin to feel worthy, because when you feel worthy, you feel good. And when you feel good, you feel beautiful. And when you feel beautiful, you are beautiful. When you feel worthy, there is no discord between your physical self and the greater non-physical part of you who inherently knows of its worthiness.

Your worth is not defined by your height, weight, beauty, or anything else related to your physical self. Your worthiness has nothing to do with what others think of you. You can only control yourself. None of us can control what others think and do.
It's all about your own thoughts about yourself.
They are *your* thoughts.
Choose to take control.

You are worthy.
Always, forever.
You are worthy.
Which makes you, in turn, worthy of.
Of anything and everything you desire.

Love Yourself

Other than a few of my closest friends who have come to expect my shenanigans, people are often a bit taken aback when I tell them, on occasion, in all honestly, "I'm fucking awesome." It usually gets a big laugh, which is what I'm expecting. But seriously, why are we so unaccustomed to praising ourselves? Self-love is crucial to building self confidence, and crucial to understanding our true nature, which is love itself. I appreciate Christian Northrup's advice: "If we can't feel good about our skills and accomplishments, no one else can, either. Find a few friends you can brag with! Send each other e-mails regularly, bragging about how wonderful and skillful you are!"

Sometimes I wonder why some people have an inherent sense of their worthiness, while others do not.
But it probably doesn't matter.
You can't teach worthiness.
You have to *allow* yourself to feel it.
You don't have to feel like you're doing something bad when you love yourself or praise yourself.
Go ahead, brag about something you feel good about.
It's not a sin.
I'd bet that God would love to hear about how much you love yourself.

Receive

Recently, I went to a party where I saw a group of old friends and acquaintances, some of whom I haven't seen since high school (read: in over 25 years). Super fun. I was talking to a woman who is always sweet and very complimentary on the rare occasions I see her. She is also always self-deprecating and has a hard time accepting a compliment. When I talk to her, I often feel almost awkward. I've accepted her compliment with a sincere "thank you," and in turn, I give her a sincere compliment. But she almost always reacts with a self-deprecating remark such as "Oh, you like my scarf? I'm only wearing it to cover my fat belly." I find myself wishing I could convince her of her worthiness, of her inherent beauty. I would love to be able to relay to her that she is beautiful, sexy, vibrant, based solely on the fact that she is a woman.

Amy Schumer made this point in an interview I heard on Fresh Air. Terri Gross was discussing Amy's relationship with a professional wrestler, and she asked Amy whether or not she felt self-conscious around him, since he had such a "fit" physique. Amy's response, to paraphrase, was, "Well, I've always felt that when a woman takes off her clothes in front of a man, no matter what kind of shape she's in, there's a certain amount of 'You're welcome,' involved."
Hilarious. And so damned true.

And my friend's inability to accept my compliment? I believe that's tied to our inability to receive, period. Being unable to receive causes so much imbalance in women's lives.
Receive compliments, receive help, receive love.
Receiving is as important as giving.

Most women are naturally inclined to give - it's a part of our instinct to nurture. Giving is wonderful, and a necessary component to a fulfilling life, happiness, and natural beauty. But many neglect the vital need we all have to receive. We consider ourselves selfish, or perhaps unworthy of receiving, and because of this, imbalance ensues.

Learn to receive...love, help, gifts, compliments, etc. If all you ever do is give, to your family, your friends, your work, eventually you will give yourself away.
Giving is good, but you have to be able to receive in return.
So the next time you someone offers you a compliment, just say thank you.
I promise you won't spontaneously combust.

https://www.youtube.com/watch?v=hzlvDV3mpZw

A High Quality No

When you live your life trying to please others, you are living an unbalanced life - always giving, never receiving. It's not your job to please someone else; it is your job to please yourself. Abraham has said, "...that would be our dominant quest: Entertaining Yourself, pleasing Yourself, connecting with Yourself, being Yourself, loving Yourself. Some say, 'Well Abraham, you teach selfishness.' And we say yes we do, yes we do, yes we do, because unless you are selfish enough to reach for that connection [to alignment with Source Energy, to feeling good], you don't have anything to give anyone, anyway. And when you are selfish enough to make that connection, you have an enormous gift to give everywhere you are."

When you come at life from this vantage point, you begin to let go of the feeling of obligation. We all do things we feel obligated to - dinner with your in-laws, volunteering at school, hosting a fundraiser, etc. etc. To be clear, you may *want* to do these things, but if you are doing something because you feel you *have to* rather than *want to*, let go of that feeling of obligation. Because how do you feel in the moment when you are doing something because you "have to" in order to please someone else? Lousy? Frustrated? Unhappy? And that's the energy that you're bringing to that moment, to that person you are trying to please. It's a lose/lose scenario.

Just don't do things that you don't want to do. Learning how to give others a "high quality no" will benefit everyone. There is nothing wrong with saying, "No thanks. That's not going to work for me." You may be surprised how open and receptive people are to your honesty. And if they're not, that's their problem, not yours.

Cultivate Confidence

Understanding your worthiness is the basis of confidence. And confidence is attractive. Beautiful, some may say. Confidence allows us to hold our heads high. Confidence is the indicator to the outer world that you recognize your worthiness. Confident people are secure. They are not jealous. They find it easy to love others, and in turn they are easy to love.

Confidence, as defined by the Merriam Webster Dictionary, "stresses faith in oneself and one's powers without any suggestion of conceit or arrogance." Feeling confident feels much better than feeling insecure, because you're connected to your true nature, Well-Being.

Feeling confident is not a feeling of superiority. Rather, it is being at ease with yourself, regardless of anyone else's opinion. It is a knowing of worthiness. An inherent understanding of your true nature. It is self-love.

From a physical perspective, confidence is often projected by good posture. Attaining good posture, whether it's inherent or learned through a practice such as yoga, is another component to allowing natural beauty.

A while ago I read an article written by a self-described "unconventionally beautiful" woman named Meg Howry.
An excerpt from that article, in which she quotes from Henry James' novel, The Europeans, reads:

"A compliment had once been paid her that, being repeated to her, gave her greater pleasure than anything she had ever heard.
'A pretty woman?' some one had said.
'Why, her features are very bad.'
'I don't know about her features,' a very discerning observer had answered, 'but she carries her head like a pretty woman.'"

Howry goes on to state, "Now, this may seem like just another version of the old confidence-as-beauty trope, but for me this was more than beauty as a state of mind: it carried an actual physical directive."

What I find so perfect about her assessment of this passage is the fact that "beauty as a state of mind" quite literally leads to the "physical directive." What begins in the mind manifests into reality.

She continues, "An insecure woman would carry her head down, apologetically, or maybe thrust it out, defiantly, but a pretty woman would carry it easily, balanced just so at the top of her neck, floating. A pretty woman is free. She can take her loveliness as a matter of course and get on with the interesting task of thinking and doing."

Pretty is a state of mind. So is insecurity. And confidence. One leads to feelings of hopelessness, effort, unworthiness. The others, relief, effortlessness, worthiness. And you can choose your state of mind. You have the choice to think thoughts that feel good, that give you relief. And those thoughts will cause a physical directive within your body, be it in the form of emotion or actual choreography.

Pay attention to what you are thinking and create the life, the state of mind, the reality that you want.

"See beauty, even when it's not pretty, every day."
~Adapted from The Invitation by Oriah Mountain Dreamer

"The Wall Is Your Guru"

~B.K.S. Iyengar

Eventually my desire to cultivate good posture led me to B.K.S. Iyengar, the creator of Iyengar yoga. While visiting my brother-and-sister-in-law in Chicago and perusing their bookshelf, I came across Light On Life, by Iyengar. I pulled it off the shelf and was immediately riveted by Iyengar's story. While I had dabbled in practicing many different types of yoga over the years, it was clear that his beliefs were in close alignment with mine. It was therefore not surprising that I began to feel curious about and interested in trying this particular practice of yoga. My desire, however, was not so strong as to prompt any action towards finding out if anyone offered a class in Milwaukee.

Within a month or so, I was in my doctor's office for a routine exam. As I stared around the room waiting for my doctor to come in (we all do that, right?), I noticed a flyer on the bulletin board for the Milwaukee Yoga Center. I looked closer and saw that MYC was an Iyengar studio, meaning only Iyengar yoga was taught there. I decided to pursue it, and soon enough was introduced to Iyengar yoga, my teachers, and another path that I have used to feel good and allow not only better posture, but better health in general.

"Yoga teaches us to cure what need not be endured and endure what cannot be cured."
~B.K.S. Iyengar

Creating Wealth Consciousness

Understanding your worthiness is also the basis for creating abundance. Of course, abundance can take any form - abundance of love, happiness, money, sunshine - but in this case, I'm talking about financial abundance. Years ago, on a boring day at work, a colleague of mine asked a group of us, "If you could have any of the following, what would you choose: wealth, a fulfilling intimate relationship, meaningful friendships, or good health?" I answered, "Well, I guess I'd choose wealth, since I have everything else." It got a big laugh, but it was actually true.

When I started this process of awakening, I had amassed a lifetime of beliefs, many of which manifested as resistance to financial abundance. I would say I suffered from a "lack consciousness" mentality, and wanted to move towards "wealth consciousness," concepts introduced to me by Bob Doyle, one of the teachers of "The Secret." That is, I wanted to embrace the belief that we are all inherently abundant and worthy of abundance, and have access to manifesting abundance beyond our wildest dreams if we only allow it. My persistent thoughts that I did not have enough money, that I was always running out of money, that I would never have enough, dominated my vibration. My monthly responsibility to pay our bills and reconcile our checkbook would inevitably end in tears, as did living paycheck-to-paycheck, month after month, year after year. I was constantly worried about money.

Developing wealth consciousness, to me, meant believing in our abundance, rather than our lack of it. I began to practice looking at all of the evidence in my life that proved our abundance, both from the spiritual perspective (my husband, my children, my family, my friends), as well as my physical surroundings and how they represented our enormous state of abundance. I acknowledged the presence of abundance in my life, and cultivated a deep sense of appreciation for it. I made lists of everything I had to appreciate from a physical standpoint, from our home, our furnishings, our clothes, to our washer, dryer, dishwasher, stove, refrigerator, even running water, electricity, and on and on. I realized that I was literally surrounded by beauty and function. This recognition, and more importantly, the appreciation that I felt, was evidence that I was moving in the direction that I desired, towards wealth consciousness.

At a certain point I realized that I needed to simplify the process of paying our bills. It seemed necessary to improve upon that feeling, since it almost always resulted in strong negative emotions. I started to take advantage of this new innovation (at the time) called "online banking." Gotta love technology.

By simplifying my process and having most of my bills paid automatically, this once daunting task became more and more effortless. Slowly but surely, I began to feel more and more relief around the subject of finances. This, in turn, allowed me to release resistance and begin to let go of my longstanding thoughts - beliefs - that were holding me back from my well-deserved abundance, abundance that we are all worthy of just by being alive.

Most people desire some form of financial abundance because financial abundance allows us a certain amount of freedom in our societal structure. From my perspective, I consider ultimate freedom the perfect definition of success: to live life completely on your own terms.

I Could If I Wanted To

There's a great game that Abraham teaches to get into a state of feeling abundant. It's called, "I could if I wanted to." Here's an example of my playing this game after I recognized some anxiety I felt about having made plans to go out to dinner two nights in a row, because I was worried about spending too much money.
I wanted to put myself into a state of allowing rather than resisting...

I love my life. I love that I can go out to dinner two nights in a row.
I could go out to eat every night of the week, if I wanted to.
I could eat at the finest restaurants and order anything off the menu, from champagne and lobster to High Life and a cheeseburger, if I wanted to.
I could spend any amount of money on anything, if I wanted to.
I could, if I wanted to.

Thinking about my choices in this way made me feel better. Instead of thinking in terms of "what can I afford," which introduced loads of resistance, I switched to "what would I do IF I WANTED TO," which released resistance. It's all about choosing to think thoughts that lean towards a better feeling. Simple as that.

Play games.
Have fun.
Feel good.

Deliberate Creation

Abraham likes to remind us that we are all "deliberate creators."

I'm <u>creating</u> abundance, because I am a <u>creator</u>.
Everyone is a <u>creator</u>.
We are all <u>creating</u>, all the time.
It's really what we're all about.
Desires are what we use to <u>create</u>.
We have desires when we're feeling good and when we're feeling bad. Which is why feeling bad is good - it's an important part of the <u>creating</u> process.
Those feelings are <u>creating</u> new desires.
Desires that are instantly <u>created</u> by Source.
"Ask and it is given," Abraham would say, and we either allow them to manifest into our experience, or we resist them with what Abraham calls "limiting beliefs."

Limiting beliefs include all thoughts and feelings of lack. They can sound something like, "I don't have enough time," or, "I'm running out of money," or "I'm not good enough." Limiting beliefs come in all shapes and sizes, on all subjects.

I try to replace my limiting beliefs with mantras, to trigger my awareness of them and move to a better feeling thought. It's what I did with my worry about my kids, if you recall, and how I got rid of that worry. I would like to replace thoughts of lack with:

Everything is always working out for us
or
I can have trust and faith that everything will work out
for us
or
paying for health insurance doesn't have to freak
me out
or
we always have more than enough
or
I'm comfortable with outrageous abundance
or
I have plenty to share because I have more than
enough and when you have more than enough you
have plenty to share.

Embrace Uncertainty

Truth be told, we have continued to accumulate debt throughout our lives. (Robert and I have had joint finances since our early 20's, so the "I" is really "we," with regards to our financial vibration.) But more importantly, in recent years we have released resistance by not feeling burdened by our debt. And in the recognition that we are feeling better around the subject of money, we know that we are moving in the right direction, towards the physical manifestation of the fulfillment of our desire for financial freedom. The idea of living our lives completely on our own terms is more than appealing. Something goes wrong in our house or with our car? No problem. Kids need new shoes? No problem. Doctor and dentist visits? No problem. Want to visit friends in Germany or Chile or anywhere else in the world?
No problem.
The clarity of what we want, coupled with the understanding that we can create whatever we want by being happy with where we are in any moment, pushes our vision forward. We don't know the "how" and we don't have to. We simply know that feeling abundant will eventually bring the manifestation of our desires.

Don't get me wrong - for years I have struggled with "how are we going to make this happen?" Years. Letting go of the need to know "how" is a challenge in and of itself, but it's also entirely necessary. Let go and let the universe guide you. Let go of the need to act and control. Let go. Let go of the "how" and embrace uncertainty. As Deepak says, "Uncertainty is where all creativity lies."

Being comfortable with embracing uncertainty is a necessary component of creating a good feeling life. Being ok with uncertainty goes hand-in-hand with letting go. Both are integral parts of creation. What you're really letting go of is fear. Fear is what holds most of us back from moving forward, whether it's with our careers, our relationships, our finances, whatever. Have trust and faith in the belief that all is well, and you'll be able to let go of fear.

There are many paths to achieving what one wants. Conventional wisdom will teach you that the only way is through hard work and effort. Abraham teaches us to "replace effort and trying with relaxing and allowing."
Doesn't that feel better?
When you feel good, you attract abundance in all forms.

For me, creating wealth is a work in progress. I continue to do my best to focus on feeling good around the subject of money, and not to worry. Years into this process, I can still find it challenging. But when I look back at how I used to feel and compare it to how I feel now, I have no doubt of my progress. And then I remind myself, most importantly, to look forward. Again, that all-important vision. I love Abraham's analogy to a journey in a car. To paraphrase, imagine if you were driving towards a destination, and the windshield was on the floor of your car. You might not get very far before "crashing and burning," so to speak. On any journey, you have to look forward, ahead. Because, crazy as it seems, the present moment is actually old news. It's what you've already created. Your thoughts, your vision, are what is to come. If you're not happy with your present moment, the best thing you can do is deny it your attention. Don't dwell upon it in your mind, and complain about it to your friends. Create something new. And when you *do* give it your attention, find something to appreciate about it, to get you to a good-feeling place. If I'm sounding like a broken record, it's because we learn through repetition. I'll say it again and again, because like anyone else, I need to constantly remind myself of this truth.

In the past, I may have looked at the current state of our finances and felt utter anxiety. I would have been fixated on the fact that our idea of financial freedom hadn't shown up yet. But I am finally coming to understand that it doesn't matter, because it is coming. Just because it's not here yet doesn't mean it doesn't exist. The goal is to be in the receptive mode, as Abraham calls it, by feeling good. Receive! Feeling good on any subject leads to manifestation. When I allow myself to look forward and know that everything I desire has already been created (Source Energy creates our desires instantly – it's up to us to allow them to manifest into our experience), I feel a sense of excited anticipation rather than fear and lack.
That's the receptive mode.
The old, "Ask and you shall receive."
Amen.

"Krishna, Buddha, and Jesus lie in the hearts of all. They are not film stars, mere idols of adulation. They are great inspirational figures whose example is there to be followed. They act as role models today.
Just as they reached Self-Realization, so may we."
~B.K.S. Iyengar

From Within

The best "make-over" show that I ever saw was on the Oprah Winfrey Show many years ago. On this particular show, Oprah had one or two typical makeover stories... change the clothes, change the hair, check out the new look. But by far the most dramatic makeover was a woman who recognized that her life needed to change in order for her appearance to improve. She began with a commitment to meditate daily. In addition, she began a process of visualization, in essence, creating a new reality for herself in her mind. Her energy began to increase, extra weight was shed, her skin began to glow, she felt younger and more vibrant. When she walked onstage to have her "after" moment, the difference was astonishing and beautiful to witness. She truly was a new woman, a natural beauty, but not because she lost weight and wore the right outfit. It was because she had made a change from within. She recognized her worthiness. She felt beautiful. Therefore she *was* beautiful. It was incredibly inspiring - one of many examples of how real change begins with our minds.

Self Care

I've learned a lot from Dr. Christianne Northrop, mostly from her book <u>Women's Bodies, Women's Wisdom</u>. I know I mentioned this earlier, but it's worth revisiting. When you're trying to move away from the habit of being self-critical, of stopping all of the self-judgment, keep this in mind:

"Think of one thing that you're proud of that you've accomplished today, this week, or this year. Feel your accomplishment(s) fully. Take it in, until it's more than just intellectual knowledge. Take yourself right into your heart."

It's like we're taught from a young age to suppress our love for ourselves - god forbid you're bragging or "full of yourself!" Why are these perceived as such dirty words? Because some priest two thousand years ago told us if was bad to love ourselves more than God, based on the false premise that we are separate from God? God is love, pure positive energy, Well-Being, the greater, non-physical part of ourselves! Be full of yourself! Fill yourself up with love for yourself! This is not a bad thing to do!
You will be giving yourself the ultimate
gift - wholeheartedness.
You are worthy.

The Lotus: What you desire you already have.

STEP SIX

Take Responsibility For Your Feelings

Be independent of the good or bad opinions of others.

~Wayne Dyer

Are you aware of the fact that you have the ability to choose how you feel? There is no greater freedom than the realization that you alone are responsible for your feelings. It is not up to someone else to make you feel good, and in the same respect, you do not have to allow anyone to make you feel bad. Blaming others for how you feel is terribly common in our society. Instead of continuing to fall into this bad habit, begin to recognize that you are responsible for your thoughts and reactions.

Taking responsibility for your own feelings empowers you - you take control because you have control. Wouldn't it be nice to reach a space where nothing anyone said to you made you feel negative about yourself? And where the negative thoughts that you tell yourself ceased to exist?

Through practice and awareness we can live our lives with less and less negative emotion. And when we do experience negative emotion, we can recognize that it will soon pass, and that it is necessary to experience some contrast in order to appreciate the Well-Being that surrounds us.

No Judgies

You are a mirror - what you think/do/are/see reflects how others treat you.
The quickest way to learn to be independent of anyone's good or bad opinions is to let go of your own judgment, towards yourself and, in turn, others.

We are our own harshest critics. Judgment leads to a downward spiral. If you judge yourself harshly, you inevitably judge others harshly as well, as we are all connected. When you don't feel your own worthiness, others around you will suffer for it.

Letting go of self-judgment is the first step towards letting go of all judgment.

The greater part of you, the nonphysical Source Energy that is your true self, is never judging you. It *knows* your worthiness. Well-Being knows only well-being. It knows that you can't do anything wrong. It is a constant stream of pure positive energy, and when you beat yourself up about something that you think you "did wrong," when you feel bad about yourself, when you think you are not worthy, you disconnect yourself from that flow of Well-Being.

Your Source only sees you in the positive light. It's why you feel so low when you feel bad about yourself, for any reason - you've pinched off your flow of that energy, you've moved to a different vibrational frequency than Source, and you *feel* it.
Re-connect, by shifting your thoughts. Connect to the vibration that is love, appreciation, compassion, ease, relief.

Use Thich Nhat Hanh's loving kindness meditation to keep you on track.
Tell it to yourself, and then wish it upon others:

May you be filled with loving kindness.
May you be well.
May you be peaceful and at ease.
May you be happy.

Love yourself. Forgive yourself. Stop judging yourself.

"Your true self...is immune to criticism, it isn't fearful of any challenge, and it feels superior to no one, because it recognizes that everyone else is the same self, the same spirit in different disguises."
~Deepak Chopra

You're In Charge

One of people's biggest complaints is the way other people make them feel. The funny thing is, other people can't *make* you feel anything. These are *your* feelings - own them. Other people are going to be, do and say whatever they want. It's up to you to learn how to react, or better yet, not react, to whatever they do. And this will be even easier when you pay attention to creating relationships that serve you. Because people are giving you what you expect of them.

If you have a friend who makes you unhappy, who you find annoying or unkind, then you are literally attracting that part of her personality from her. By dwelling on what you do not like about her, she pretty much has no choice but to act that way towards you. Start thinking about her in a positive light. Find something about her that you can appreciate. And that is what you will attract from her going forward. It may take some time to turn the momentum of thought from one direction to another. And you may find that maybe you don't spend as much time with that person as you once did. Or maybe your friendship will slip away all together, especially if you're not able to find anything to appreciate (and why have a friend like that, for goodness sake?). All of that is as it should be. Because you, by focusing your thoughts on only what serves you, will be allowing only that which you want to see into your experience.

People respond to your expectations of them. Your thoughts about a person in your life will affect how they act in your presence. You are the creator of your reality - good and bad. If someone is treating you in a manner that you don't appreciate, it ultimately has more to do with you and what you're expecting of them, than it does with them. You are attracting that behavior based on your thoughts about that person.

Take this example: You have a friend who you believe is intense and harsh. Since this is how you view them, this is how they will act towards you. These are the traits you are drawing from them - it's how you perceive them, so that's how they are. To *you*. Chances are, they have other people in their life that don't feel that way about them, and those people have a completely different perception and experience. It's *your* energy, *your* thoughts, that attract the behaviors of those you encounter.
It's not up to other people to change in order to accommodate you - it's up to you to change your thoughts about them.

Don't Make An Ass out of U and Me

The third of <u>The Four Agreements</u> by Don Miguel Ruiz: don't make assumptions. Sound advice. Why do we ever presume to know what someone else is thinking? Really, that's what we're doing when we make assumptions – we're thinking we know what someone else is thinking.

I've been living with Robert for over 20 years, and I've known him since kindergarten. Yet we would both agree that I can't read his mind, and vice versa. I can't read his, or my mom's, or my best friend's, or a random acquaintance's, or a complete stranger's, or anyone's mind. When we make assumptions, essentially we are believing that we are mind readers. Which is pretty silly when you look at it from that perspective, unless you happen to be blessed with that gift.

So if you're going to make an assumption, at least don't believe that it's true. And if you're going to believe that it's true, at least make sure it's positive. Because I've got a theory about assumptions:
if your assumption makes you feel bad, it's probably wrong.

The next time someone looks at you funny, don't assume they're thinking something bad or mean about you, and jump to the conclusion that you did something wrong, or that they're an asshole. Instead, think, "She must really like the way my hair looks today." Or don't think anything at all. Because you really don't know what's going on in her head, and chances are, whatever it is, it has nothing to do with you.

The Now

We are so quick to blame other people for the way we feel. This isn't all that surprising, given that blame is just a way to deflect our own pain and discomfort. This is obvious when you look at the behavior of young children. If they know they've done something wrong, or made a mistake, they will often quickly try to blame someone else. All they're doing is trying to release the pain and discomfort that their actions have caused them to feel. You come to expect this from a child who is still learning to navigate life, but it's astounding when you realize how often adults use this defense mechanism as well. Blame is all around us. It's my husband's fault that I feel like shit. It's my mother's fault that I feel like shit. Because someone did this to me my life sucks. You get the picture.
And it's all poppycock.

Guess whose "fault" it is if you feel like shit or your life isn't what you'd like it to be? Yours. Only yours. But really, there is no "fault." Your life is what it is. You haven't done anything wrong. Once you own up to the pain and discomfort that is a part of our lives, there is no more "fault," because there ceases to be a reason for any blame. Emotions are necessary - the suppression of them is the definition of depression, according to Freud. Embrace your vulnerability. It's a part of our human experience. And the knowledge that your thoughts create your reality, and that you can change your reality by managing your thoughts, will greatly reduce the amount of pain and discomfort in your life. When you begin to use the law of attraction to your advantage, fewer circumstances will arise that cause you to feel pain.

Of course, pain is not entirely avoidable, nor would we want it to be. We have to experience negative emotion in order to appreciate feeling good, to define what we want, and to begin the process of creation. But pain won't have as much power if you don't feed it. When you continue to tell the story of what went wrong, when you try to figure out why something went wrong, when you aren't able to let go of the thing that felt wrong, you're continuing to activate that vibration. You're feeding your pain. And when you feed something that much, guess what happens? It grows.

It's not that your pain wasn't or isn't valid - you may have experienced trauma, something that caused great pain and discomfort in your life, your marriage, your childhood, whenever. But if it's not happening right now, in this moment, you have the power to let it go, to move forward and not re-enact all of the negative emotions by telling the story again and again. Create a new story, and let go of the past. Like Eckhart Tolle teaches, all of your power is in the present moment, the now.

Shut the Front Door

I discussed this earlier, but it's worth noting Dr. Northrop's views on complaining again: "[W]omen shoot themselves in the foot by complaining too much. It's a bad habit. Find friends who have to courage to consciously break it."

Complaining will only ever bring you more things to complain about. It will never be a solution to a problem. As Abraham and many others teach, focusing on any problem will never bring you the solution. You have to shift your focus to finding a solution, if it's actually something you want to fix. (I make that point, because chronic complainers really seem to not want to fix their problems - and they will find anything to complain about. Steer clear from that toxicity!)

When you complain, you activate the vibration of how the thing you're complaining about made you feel. And the law of attraction responds to that vibration. So you get more of that feeling, and more circumstances that trigger that feeling. It's a vicious cycle, and very avoidable. It makes no sense to complain about anything, ever, when you see it in this light (unless you prefer to feel like shit).

Recognize all of the stories you tell about things that have happened to you, people who have wronged you, bad things that have happened to you, etc. As difficult as it may be to accept, none of these things could have happened if you didn't have an active vibration seeking out those circumstances. And your repeating the story of it continues to activate that vibration, and guess what happens? More of the same.

Break the cycle. Stop complaining. Stop re-telling the bad feeling stories. Learn to shut the fuck up, and start dwelling on the good things in your life instead of the bad. I can't tell you how often I still have to tell myself to shut the fuck up. But it's less than it used to be, so I know I'm getting somewhere. Because if re-telling the story brings you back to the feeling of negative emotion that you experienced when the circumstance happened, it's just not worth it.
Shut. The. Fuck. Up.

True Love

Robert and I were married by a Justice of the Peace in 1999. Unlike in a religious ceremony, it was up to us to tell her what to say, so we wrote our own vows and created the ceremony. I stumbled upon a hard copy of our vows recently, and have to admit, was kind of blown away by how spot-on they felt, almost 20 years later.

A reading from our wedding:

An excerpt from "A Night Among the Pines," by Robert Louis Stevenson

"…and yet even while I was exalting in my solitude I became aware of a strange lack. I wished for a companion to lie near me in the starlight, silent and not moving, but ever within touch. For there is a fellowship more quiet than solitude, and which, rightly understood, is solitude made perfect. And to live…with the woman a man loves is of all lives the most complete and free."

While being married to someone who is on the same spiritual path as you is most certainly a blessing, there are some challenges to overcome. Robert has been the greatest influence on my understanding of the importance of releasing judgment and taking responsibility for your own feelings, lessons that I have found are among the hardest for us to learn.

Robert is able to subtly point out my judgment of myself, others, circumstances, whatever, in the most sincerely nonjudgmental way.
He walks the walk.

(The thought of his walk gives me butterflies. 23 years later? That's love.)

So who better to teach me to take responsibility for my own feelings, than this man who I love so deeply? It hasn't been a breeze, but it has been enlightening. Like many others, I was quick to blame him when I was feeling down. ("You did [something] that made me feel bad.") At a certain point, he stopped accepting the blame, and I was forced to look inward. In those moments, I wanted my feeling bad to be his fault. I wanted it to be anyone's fault but my own, but no one else is in control of my feelings.
If I feel bad, I have no one to blame but myself.

Accepting this truth is actually quite liberating. And of course, it works both ways. I realized that I no longer had to feel responsible for his happiness. As a stay-at-home mom (for the most part - I work outside the home part-time), I sometimes felt guilty that he had to "punch a clock" forty hours a week. But under this premise, guilt is yet another emotion that makes no sense. (Chalk it up there with blame, obligation and judgment.) This is the life that I created for myself, and that is the life that he created for himself. And we're exactly where we are supposed to be. The happier I am, the easier I am to live with, so why not focus on my own happiness? We influence each other's vibrations, certainly, but when it comes down to it, we cannot change other people's thoughts, feelings, or behaviors. That part is up to them.

Robert and I fight occasionally. We recognize that we are human. But we don't blame each other for how we feel, and we don't expect the other to "make me feel better." Robert has helped me realize that when I feel down, there is nothing he can do to make me feel better. He could bend over backwards trying to

do the right thing, and it would have no effect on me. Whatever he might do in an effort to make me feel better would, in my depressed/frustrated/angry state of mind, feel wrong to me. Which is why, when you're trying to please people, you often feel "you're damned if you do and damned if you don't." Best to not even try. Best to put your energy into maintaining your own alignment, and wait for the other person to find theirs. I always do, eventually, and I appreciate Robert all the more for the lessons he helps me understand.
True Love.

"In my life, I love you more."
~Lennon/McCartney

STEP SEVEN

Laugh Often

Every time you smile at someone, it is an action
of love, a gift to that person, a beautiful thing.

~Anonymous

(According to random people on the Internet,
Mother Teresa said this.
Turns out, she didn't. But it's still a great quote.)

How do you feel when you have the giggles?

How do you feel when you see someone dear who you haven't seen in a while, and you burst into laughter?

How do you feel when something has made you laugh so hard, you cry?
I love describing that situation to children. I remember when my daughter saw that happen to someone, and she was worried, assuming that since that person was crying, she was sad.
"Not at all!" I explained. "She is crying because she's happy!
Those are happy tears!"
(It was probably my friend Joanna - she cries almost every time she laughs.)

Laughter = Happiness

Happy feels good. It feels so darn good. Happy is a great way to feel.

Which is why Abraham teaches us the idea of "unconditional happiness."

Be happy, regardless of your conditions.

Conditions, Schmonditions

Feel good regardless of the conditions surrounding you.

What a concept!
Typically, we rely on our conditions to find happiness.
Be it good weather, lots of money, the perfect spouse -
life is full of conditions.

When you choose to be happy regardless of "what is,"
you are unconditionally happy. You see that happiness
can only come from within yourself. The outside world
doesn't need to have anything to do with how you feel.
And the bonus is, when you make the choice to be
unconditionally happy,
chances are, you will have a lot in life to be happy
about.

Choose to be unconditionally happy. Let everything
else off the hook.

When you're on vacation, and you're sitting on a
beach, staring into a beautiful body of water, watching
your children play in the sand, you say, "This is the life!"

And it is. This is the life. Regardless of that time off from
work, that warm sunshine on your face, that feeling of
ease. You can have that feeling whenever and wherever.
You don't need to go on a vacation to reach that place.
Your life, in general, is "the life." It has led you to that
place of sitting on a beach, feeling that way,
appreciating.
You have created that moment.
So keep creating.
Make it easy, good, effortless, fun, abundant,
happy.

Pro-Living

In my mind, anti-aging equates to pro-dying-young.
The anti-aging industry - created to resist the inevitable
and natural process of aging - makes no sense to me.
Mind you, I have no issue with the products themselves,
or people's desire to use them if it makes them feel
good. But I do think they would have a better effect
if they were marketed from an "age gracefully"
perspective instead. I suppose that's because "aging
gracefully" feels better to me than "anti-aging."

Aging gracefully is nothing more than continued
acceptance and love for yourself.
As you grow older and you
continue to,
choose to,
learn to
love and accept yourself,
you age gracefully.

I'm a woman in my mid-forties who is feeling the onset
of peri-menopause, so I've given the topic of aging
and the changes that come with it a fair amount of
thought recently. And I've come to a realization:
Aging does not scare me.
I intend to age gracefully. Supported by this intention,
I will do my best to ignore conventional wisdom's
assumption that our bodies and minds inevitably decline
and deteriorate as we get older. Have you ever searched
YouTube for "80 year old woman doing yoga" or Google
for "how old is Gloria Steinem?"(She's in her eighties and
is as active and vibrant and beautiful as ever.) You may
be surprised to find out that there are a plethora (yes,
a plethora) of beautiful, old women doing all sorts of
amazing things with their bodies and their minds.

Yes, our bodies change as we age. They change. But they do not necessarily deteriorate. Yet, it's no wonder that many bodies do, indeed, deteriorate, given that when it comes to the topic of aging in our society, there are considerably fewer folks who choose to view the process in a positive light.

"Getting old is a bitch?" Fuck that.

When I contemplate aging, I do my best to tell myself the following:

I would like to age with vitality.

I intend to age gracefully.

I look forward to a healthy body and mind in my old age.

I look forward to experiencing life from the perspective of one who has lived many years and gained much wisdom.

Bring on the crows feet, the wrinkles, the laugh lines - they are a sign of a life worth living.

Something To Laugh About

Ever find yourself referring to something you think is really great as "to die for?" It's a common expression. I have a friend, a two-time cancer survivor, who chooses to say, "to live for" instead. And I follow suit, because I'd rather live for it than die for it.

But keep in mind - we are simultaneously physical and non-physical beings. The physical aspect of ourselves - our bodies - allows the greater, non-physical part of ourselves to experience life, humanity. This thing we call death is really only death of the physical, the body. The greater part of us has always been and will always be non-physical, energy. Our bodies croak, as Abraham likes to say (because why not treat death lightly, if we really don't die?), and we re-emerge fully as pure positive energy, where only Well-Being, love, joy, bliss, abides. Without a doubt, grief is felt physically, but as far as the person who has left the building is concerned?
They are all good.
Couldn't be happier.
Laughing all the way to the grave.

There is a character in John Greene's book, <u>Looking For Alaska</u>, a teenager nick-named Pudge. A wise kid, that one. His reflections resonated with me - it's one of the best passages from a novel I've ever read:

"...When adults say, 'Teenagers think they are invincible' with that sly, stupid smile on their faces, they don't know how right they are. We need never be hopeless, because we can never be irreparably broken. We think that we are invincible because we are. We cannot be born, and we cannot die. Like all energy, we can only change shapes and sizes and manifestations. They forget that when they get old. They get scared of losing and failing. But that part of us greater than the sum of our parts cannot begin and cannot end, and so it cannot fail."

Thanks for that, Mr. Greene.

"The opposite of death is birth. Life has no opposite."
~Eckhart Tolle

It's Not Just Another Organ

The Institute of Heartmath has made many fascinating discoveries regarding the human heart. (This was another topic that I was introduced to while watching Tom Shadrach's documentary, "I Am.") So many of us believe that the brain is the epicenter of the body, that it is the one in charge. Turns out, not so much. The heart, in fact, is telling the brain what to do, way more than the other way around. "The heart is the boss of us," said one scientist.

Among a bunch of other really cool things, these scientists have proven that feeling compassion actually renews our physiology. We are designed to operate optimally in states of love and appreciation. It makes perfect sense, considering when we feel love and appreciation, we are aligning with the greater, non-physical part of ourselves that IS love and appreciation.

I've learned that I feel happy when I take time to focus on my heart. When I close my eyes and put my attention on my heart, it feels good. I breathe in and picture my heart expanding, and breathe out, contracting. I feel the flow of blood and information flowing through my body. I pay attention to the beauty that is my heart, and I feel the wisdom that is being communicated with every heartbeat. I feel my body fill with a loving energy. I feel aligned with Source Energy. I feel good.
Go ahead and try it someday.
See how you feel.
Your heart will show it's appreciation, I bet, and you'll see what I'm talking about.

Groundhog Day

Ever notice how some people will flee from an
unpleasant condition, only to find themselves right
back in the unpleasant condition, over and over
again? We'll think to ourselves,
"Well, maybe I should move, since I am so unhappy
<u>here</u>."
"Maybe I should find a new job, because I am
unhappy with <u>this</u> job."
"Maybe I should leave my husband,
because it's his fault that <u>I'm</u> unhappy."

Just remember:
"You take yourself with you."
Abraham taught me that. Unless you clean up your
own vibrational baggage, you will repeat that process
again and again. You'll move, and still feel unhappy.
You'll find a new job, and you won't like that one either.
Divorce your husband, and marry another man just
like him.
You take yourself with you.
Find peace within yourself, shift your vibration, break
the pattern.

Joy To the World

Marie Kondo's catchphrase, "Spark Joy," makes me so happy, I can't stand it. What a brilliant concept! If you've been living under a rock and haven't heard of her (no judgies!), go ahead and Google it, buy her book, and get with the program.

Joy, appreciation, love - they are all the same vibration. Strong emotions, strong vibrations. See them for what they are: powerful tools of creation. Your heart generates a measurable magnetic field that can be detected by other people's brains. When you feel good, you not only renew your own physiology, but you affect those around you in a positive way.
Keep laughing. Spread your joy.

Last But Not Least...

Pay attention to the evidence.

You are surrounded by evidence of your thoughts. The fun part is recognizing all of the evidence, especially once you begin to create the life you actually want. A coincidence is merely evidence of the law of attraction at work. You are a co-creator of your life experience. Evidence will come in many shapes and forms. It's up to you to notice it and appreciate it, as thoughts of appreciation are one of the most powerful positive vibrations that one can emit.

I see evidence around me all the time. Abraham has a saying,
"It's as easy to create a castle as it is a button."
One morning as I was out walking, I was reflecting on that saying. I thought to myself that I had never, in fact, created a button. So, I decided to give it a go, and threw the intention to create a button into the universe.
I let it go.
Forgot all about it, in fact, since I wasn't really that attached to it.
(Like I *am* attached to, say, creating a Tesla. Which hasn't manifested for me yet, because I'm too focused on the fact that I don't have it.
See how this works?)
A few weeks later, I was at a work-related gathering, where people were receiving prizes if their business cards were picked out of a bowl...like a raffle. One of the prizes was a handful of sample buttons for shirts and sportcoats - a tool to use when meeting clients to show them their options. Guess who won them? Not one button, a bunch. That's evidence.

And it doesn't have to be quite that dramatic!
Evidence of your thoughts manifesting reality is *everywhere*. I recognize it in so many ways, like running

144

into someone who I had just thought of yesterday. Or hearing a song on the radio that I was singing earlier that day. I consider finding a quarter on the street evidence of my abundance. We experience these little coincidences every day, all the time. They are all around us. Go ahead and make it into a game.
Pay attention to the evidence of the manifestations of your thoughts.
And do your best to choose thoughts that feel good.

Feel good when you eat chocolate, feel good when you spend money, feel good when you do housework, feel good when you look in the mirror. The more you practice feeling good, the easier your life will become.

And remember that we are also here to experience contrast. Negative emotion is a part of our lives. Be ok with it, be aware of it, but do your best not to dwell in it. Recognize the "pain body" that Eckhart Tolle teaches us about in <u>A New Earth</u>. The pain body wants nothing more than to keep you in a place of feeling bad. When you become aware that this is happening, remind yourself that it actually feels good to feel good. And if you want to believe that feeling bad feels good for the moment, then go ahead and feel the negative emotion, knowing that it will pass quickly if you let it.

Things happen in our lives that we do not want. It's very rare for someone to be able to exist with zero negativity. We must have contrast, or negative emotion, in order to experience life and expand. Contrast brings us clarity. It brings a deeper understanding of what it is we truly want. Negative emotion can suck, but it really is necessary. The shift occurs when you recognize it for what it is, even in the midst of it, and appreciate it. When you're sad, it's worth telling yourself, "Damn, I feel sad. I feel sad now, but soon enough I will feel better.

And I know that this feeling of sadness is sparking new desires, allowing myself and the entire universe to expand. So I'm ok with feeling sad for now."

Shift your awareness back to the feeling of relief,
to thoughts that bring you relief,
and step back into the flow of Well-Being that is always there.
You are either allowing or resisting it, but it is always there.
What you resist persists.
And what you focus on grows.
Pay attention.
Feel good.

There's a lot of stuff in the world that makes us feel bad. Murder. War. Famine. Disease. In fact it's possible that just reading those words gave you a sick feeling in your stomach.
Writing them sure did for me.
So why pay so much attention to these subjects?
We are inundated with information in this day and age, but you have a choice as to how much information you allow yourself to focus on each day. I choose not to pay attention to too much of it, because I'm not interested in sacrificing my alignment with Well-Being in order to feel informed.
I'd rather feel good.

People may think I'm ignorant. I'm ok with that.
(Be independent of the good or bad opinions of others, right?)
I believe that I have a greater effect on world peace by looking away from the heavy stuff in the world. (I stopped watching the news so many years ago, I can't even remember when it was.) When I focus on feeling good, that's the vibration I give to the universe. When

people are suffering, I want to focus on their Well-Being, because I know it is there. I love knowing that we, as people, are all so different, and those differences are completely necessary. I love that some people feel that they should be "armed with information," and I love knowing that I shouldn't be.
The way I see it, that's not ignorance.
That's experience.

Bringing your awareness to subjects that you do not want draws those subjects into your experience. Being anti-anything allows the "anti" to grow by your focus on it alone.

And while I recognize that others feel it's necessary to focus on that which they are not wanting, I often wonder...
What good has come from all of our attention on things we do not want?
Are there fewer wars now that we can watch them on live television?
Has our health gotten better with all of our focus on disease?
I wish.

I do wish. That's what I want for the world. Peace, love, understanding, appreciation of everything and everyone.
Our vibrations can be affected by our collective consciousness, when we're not paying attention. So I've found that paying attention to my thoughts and feelings is worth the effort.

"The Age of Aquarius is causing great turmoil, to make room for the new values of love, brotherhood, unity and integrity. Everything with Piscean values is being exposed and taken down. This includes governments, corporations, individuals, and even personal relationships. Many call this a disaster, as the world appears to be falling apart, but is it?

The Aquarian Age points to the direction of our own evolution in consciousness. We are each being asked to make a choice. We can cling to the old outdated values or adopt the new evolving ones. Our happiness and peace depends on our choice. The change will take place whether we like it or not."
~Sandra Weaver

Let's create more happiness, peace, and natural beauty in the world.

Feel beauty full.

"He who seeks beauty will find it."
~Bill Cunningham

Acknowledgments

I'd like to thank Esther and Jerry Hicks for sharing Abraham with the world. Also, Abraham, for their great love of humanity.

Thank you, Joanna Dane, Betsy Hemm, Monica Maniaci, Kris Slugg, Lindsey Ashlock, Catherine Koons-Hubbard, Debra Pyne and Adrienne Pierluissi for your encouragement, critique, editing and artistic collaboration.

Thank you, Oprah Winfrey, for introducing me to my most influential teachers, including Maya Angelou, Elie Wiesel, Deepak Chopra, Jill Bolte Taylor, Eckhart Tolle, Christianne Northrop and Abraham, to name just a few.

Mom and Dad, thank you for your unconditional love and support throughout my life.
My thanks to Jonathan, my big brother, forever there for me when I need him. Satyagraha.

Lola and Harper, thanks for being the coolest people ever.
I love you to pieces.

And most of all, thank you,
Robert,
for being my guru,
my zen master,
my partner,
lover,
and very best friend.
Here's to our adventure without risk.

67319681R00101

Made in the USA
Lexington, KY
08 September 2017